a sweet life without sugar

My deepest appreciation to the following people: Design by Nancy Campana: www.campanadesign.com. Photos by Louis Lesko: www.louislesko.com and Marilyn Caven, who can be reached at finefoto@sonic.net. Typesetting by Bill Schwartz, Resolution Graphics, resolution-graphics.com. Printed in China.

# a sweet life without sugar

NATURALLY SUGAR-FREE & GLUTEN-FREE RECIPES

Joan Miller

# contents

# Welcome to a Sweet Life

A sweet life without the sugar is finally yours, so indulge in these delicious desserts made with natural, low-glycemic sweeteners and gluten-free grains. They bring comfort and gratification without the worry. Now everyone can enjoy the taste of traditional desserts, without the risks associated with sugar and gluten.

Whether you have concerns such as diabetes or celiac disease or simply want to improve your health and feel better, you can now create outstanding desserts that you are proud to share.

A remarkable bonus is that a small serving satisfies, without the harmful cravings which accompany most sugary desserts.[1]

In *A Sweet Life Without Sugar*, you'll benefit from my years of experience with sugar-free and gluten-free desserts. I'll share my most popular recipes, my secrets for success, and my list of the finest ingredients. Beginning with the simpler recipes in the Beginning Recipes section, you'll soon be celebrating life with scrumptious healthy desserts.

## Low Glycemic – Naturally

The glycemic value of a food refers to its effect on blood sugar levels. Low-glycemic carbohydrates enter the bloodstream slowly, resulting in more stable blood sugar levels, improved energy, and better moods.

The recipes in this book were created to meet people's varying health needs and tastes. The flavor and texture of your finished desserts will depend upon the sweeteners used and your choice of ingredients (see section: Choice Ingredients).

(Diabetic Alert: If you are diabetic, using low-glycemic sweeteners instead of sugar may improve your blood sugar levels and alter your oral hypoglycemic or insulin requirements. Contact your health care provider before starting a new food, exercise or stress-reduction program.)

## Best Sweeteners

### Stevia: A Sweet-Lover's Dream

People are always looking for safe sugar substitutes. *Stevia Rebaudiana*, an herb in the sunflower family, has a long track record and in its natural form is probably the best and safest of all the sweeteners. The stevia plant is native to Paraguay, where it has been used for centuries. Although it has no calories or carbohydrates, the leaves of the stevia plant taste extremely sweet—hundreds of times sweeter than sugar.

Many people are beginning to grow this herb in their home gardens. A freshly-picked leaf will sweeten a pot of tea. In Japan, China, Germany, Malaysia, Israel and South Korea, stevia has been used as a sweetener for many years. In the U.S. it is swiftly gaining popularity.

Some studies are questioning the safety of stevia; it's important to note that this research has been done on products using only one part of the stevia leaf. Because the whole leaf has a long history of safe usage, I recommend using only the whole leaf extract of stevia in my recipes.

### Health Benefits of Stevia

- Treats diabetes[2]
- Does not affect blood sugar
- Reduces bacteria in the mouth, which can lead to tooth decay and gum disease[3]
- Calorie-free[4]
- 100% natural
- May kill cold and flu germs in the mouth[5]
- Heat stable
- No known side effects
- Used for 100's of years
- No adverse affects when tested on animals and humans

### Shopping for Stevia

Stevia is processed in many different ways to yield a variety of commercial products. You might see it sold as dried leaves, green powder, white powder, clear liquid or dark liquid. Some manufacturers use only one part of the leaf; others use the entire leaf. Depending on how it is processed, it might be sold with other sweeteners or in the supplement or herb section of your market. With so many choices, it can be confusing, so let me guide you.

When a recipe calls for stevia, I use pure white powdered stevia made from the entire stevia leaf. My favorite is NuStevia Pure White Stevia Extract™ by NuNaturals Company. NuNaturals, as well as other brands, can now be found in many markets or ordered from **www.asweetlifewithoutsugar.com**.

Because stevia is extremely sweet, use it carefully, as too much may taste bitter. Some people complain of a licorice flavor, but high-grade stevia, which is grown and processed carefully, does not have an aftertaste.

Because it is such a concentrated sweetener, some companies add flowing agents to disperse the stevia when it's sprinkled on foods.

The recipes in this book contain pure stevia powder. Read labels carefully. Products with flowing agents will give less sweetness, so you will have to adjust the amount used. If you prefer, you can purchase liquid stevia; measure it as you would the pure stevia powder and stir it into any liquid ingredient in the recipe.

The stevia product market is new and quickly expanding. To keep up to date on new products or changes to the recipes, visit **www.asweetlifewithoutsugar.com**.

## Yacon Syrup: The Wonder Sweetener

Yacon is a root vegetable, traditionally grown in the Andes of South America. A low-glycemic sweetener, its popularity among diabetics and dieters is growing. Rich in an indigestible sugar called fructooligosaccharide or FOS, yacon adds sweetness with fewer calories. FOS is considered a prebiotic, because it feeds healthy colon bacteria, improves digestion and boosts immune function.

The root can be dried and ground into a sweet powder or made into syrup using an evaporator. Because it is not heated above 110° in this process, it is considered a raw food, filled with enzymes. In taste, yacon syrup most closely resembles molasses or brown sugar.

*Health Benefits of Yacon*

- Low calorie
- Low glycemic [6]
- Recommended for diabetics [7]
- Aids digestion
- Strengthens the immune system
- Good for athletes
- Gives consistent energy
- Helps with weight loss [8]

*Shopping for Yacon*

Yacon is available at some health-conscious markets and may also be purchased online in jars, bottles or gallon jugs. See: **www.asweetlifewithoutsugar.com** for ordering instructions, or ask your local market to stock this valuable food. The recipes in this book have been formulated using yacon syrup instead of powdered yacon.

## Erythritol: A Valuable Sweetener

Erythritol is a sweet-tasting polyol that is found naturally in grapes, pears, mushrooms, soy sauce, some cheeses, wine and beer. It is made by breaking starch into glucose, fermenting it into erythritol, which is then purified to 99.5 percent. Although it is considered a sugar alcohol, erythritol does not act as a sugar or an alcohol in the body. It has been used for years in diet and low-carbohydrate foods. In 1999 the World Health Organization (WHO/FAO) Joint Expert Committee on Food Additives (JECFA) reviewed the safety of erythritol and gave it the highest safety category possible.[9]

Petitions have been submitted to additional governmental agencies throughout the world to expand the use of erythritol. It has already been approved for use in food in more than 20 jurisdictions including Canada, Mexico, Australia and the European Union.

Up to 90% of ingested erythritol is absorbed into the small intestine and excreted unchanged in the urine within twenty-four hours. This means that unlike other sugar alcohols such as xylitol or sorbitol, erythritol does not cause gas, bloating or diarrhea in most people. Those with irritable bowel syndrome or digestive problems may experience some gaseous or laxative side effects if using more than one gram per day. The recipes in this book combine erythritol with stevia or yacon, so a serving contains relatively small amounts of erythritol. Erythritol can have a slightly cool feeling on the tongue. It works well to use it along with pure stevia powder in the recipes.

*Health Benefits of Erythritol*

- Low calorie and low carbohydrate
- Natural sweetener
- Zero glycemic index (Does not raise insulin or affect blood sugar.)[10]
- Looks like sugar and is about 70% as sweet
- Declared by the FDA to be GRAS (Generally Recognized as Safe)
- Good for teeth because it doesn't feed bacteria
- Makes the mouth more alkaline, which can inhibit plaque buildup
- Generally does not create gas and bloating
- Has no aftertaste
- Increases the shelf-life of foods

*Shopping for Erythritol*

Look for 100% pure erythritol. Some recipes in this book combine stevia and erythritol. Products such as Truvia™ combine erythritol and stevia, but use only one part of the stevia leaf. Since the whole stevia leaf has been used as a sweetener for more than 1500 years without complaints, I recommend using pure erythritol and pure 100% stevia instead of Truvia™.

## Avoid These Sweeteners

### Agave

Many people use agave nectar, believing it is a safe and healthy alternative to sugar. A closer examination of agave reveals that it can have very high concentrations of fructose, possibly higher than high-fructose corn syrup (HFCS). New research reveals the dangers of consuming too much high-fructose corn syrup.[11] Although HFCS doesn't raise insulin levels, fructose can contribute to insulin resistance or type 2 diabetes.[12]

Nectar doesn't flow from the plant as the name implies, but comes from exposing the root to various chemicals and enzymes, producing highly-refined fructose syrup.[13] Some companies produce agave nectar from organic plants treated with natural enzymes and processed at low temperatures, but the product is still 70% fructose. This can be a problem unless only a very small quantity is consumed each day.

*Problems with Agave*

- May cause weight gain[14]
- May put undue stress on vital organs[15]
- May increase uric acid levels in the body[16]
- May contribute to diabetes[17]
- May come from inferior plant strains
- May contain pesticides

### Fructose

Fructose is a simple sugar found in many foods, such as honey, fruit, and some root vegetables. It is also found in high-fructose corn syrup and agave nectar. Dried and crystallized, it looks like table sugar, but is sweeter.

In the 40 years since the introduction of high-fructose corn syrup as a cost-effective sweetener in the American diet, rates of obesity in the U.S. have skyrocketed, according to the Centers for Disease Control and Prevention.[18]

*Problems with Fructose*

- May contribute to obesity[19]
- May contribute to high blood pressure[20]
- May contribute to kidney disease[21]
- May contribute to insulin resistance[22]
- May cause increased hunger[23]
- May cause increased uric acid levels in the body[24]
- May contribute to inflammation[25]

### Artificial Sweeteners

Aspartame and Sucralose can seriously disturb the delicate communication in the body's biochemistry. Ironically, the chaos they create in the cells can increase the risk of obesity and be detrimental to overall health.

**Aspartame**: Nutrasweet,™ Equal,™ Amino-Sweet™, and Neotame™ are all brand names for aspartame. Currently used in over 6000 products, the evidence about aspartame's dangers is compelling. Many side effects have been reported from the use of aspartame. Ten percent of aspartame is composed of methyl or wood alcohol. When heated, this breaks down into formaldehyde, a known carcinogen. Documented reactions to aspartame include headaches, dizziness, seizures, nausea, numbness, muscle spasms, weight gain, rashes, depression, fatigue, irritability, tachycardia, insomnia, vision problems, hearing loss, heart palpitations, breathing difficulties, anxiety attacks, slurred speech, loss of taste, tinnitus, vertigo, memory loss, and joint pain.[26]

**Sucralose**: In spite of clever marketing campaigns that say it is natural, ("Made from sugar so it tastes like sugar") Splenda™, the brand name for sucralose, is a chemically-created product and does not appear in nature.

### Other Sweeteners to Avoid

The following sweeteners are not recommended, because they affect blood sugar, feed microbes or are difficult to digest:

- Honey
- Brown rice syrup
- Xylitol
- Raw cane sugar
- Maple syrup
- Palm sugar

## Why Gluten-Free?

Gluten intolerance is four times more prevalent than it was in the 1950's, according to research at Mayo Clinic.[27] It can take the form of an allergy, an intolerance or the more serious celiac disease.

An allergy to wheat or gluten causes an immediate response, such as hives, sneezing, runny nose, teary eyes, or stomach pain. If the allergy is to wheat only, and not to all gluten, the person can eat other grains containing gluten with no problem.

Gluten intolerance or non-celiac gluten sensitivity (NCGS) means a person has celiac-like symptoms, though blood tests are negative. According to Dr Scot Lewey, as many as 10-30% of the US population is gluten-intolerant.[28]

Celiac disease affects one in 100 people worldwide,[29] though it is often undiagnosed or misdiagnosed. It is a serious autoimmune disease, causing the body to attack the lining of the small intestine. Symptoms are numerous, including gas, stomach pain, diarrhea, depression, ADHD, dental and bone disorders, joint pain, rashes, tingling in the legs and feet, and anemia.

> … undiagnosed or 'silent' celiac disease may have a significant impact on survival. The increasing prevalence, combined with the mortality impact, suggests celiac disease could be a significant public health issue, says Joseph Murray, MD, who led the study for the Mayo Clinic. [30]

Because symptoms are so diverse and blood tests often inconclusive, it makes good sense to eliminate gluten from the diet for at least three weeks to see if symptoms improve. This book shows you how easy and delicious it is to eat gluten-free desserts.

The word gluten is derived from the Greek word for glue. Gluten gives baked goods their soft chewy texture, making them our "comfort foods." In the digestive tract, gluten is sticky and tends to clog up the intestinal walls, blocking the ability to absorb nutrients from food. Undigested gluten can trigger the immune system to attack the lining of the small intestine, causing distress. [31]

It's important to be aware that today's wheat is grown to be higher in gluten. Historically people mixed wheat with other grains, seeds and nuts, but today we've been raised to prefer the soft texture of refined high-gluten wheat.

### Gluten Grains

| | |
|---|---|
| Wheat | Spelt |
| Rye | Some oats |
| Barley | Kamut |

### Gluten-Free

| | |
|---|---|
| Rice | Corn |
| Quinoa | Artichoke |
| Tapioca | Arrowroot |
| Amaranth | Sorghum |
| Buckwheat | Tree nut |
| Teff | Coconut |
| Bean | Certified oats |
| Millet | Kuzu |

## Best Flours for Best Results

I recommend using the flour blend recipe on page 17. It has superior nutrition and works well in a variety of dishes. Combining flours helps prevent the dessert from becoming overpowered by one taste or texture. A small amount of xanthan gum is added to the flour blend to improve the texture of your baked goods.

If you choose to buy a flour blend, a variety of them are sold online and in health-conscious markets. Ingredients vary, so experiment with several to see which ones you prefer. I avoid using white rice flour or potato starch, since both lack quality nutrition. Be sure to read labels, as some blends are sweetened. If you must use only one kind of flour, I recommend brown rice or sorghum flour.

## Flour Freshness Tips

The higher oil content in unrefined flours makes them extremely perishable. Air, light, heat and moisture can easily cause mold and rancidity. Insect infestation can also be a problem.

Store your flours in glass jars or food-grade plastic containers with tight-fitting lids, or better yet, vacuum pack them. It's best to keep them frozen or refrigerated. If you don't have room for this, choose a cool, dry, dark place and use or discard after several weeks.

## Choice Ingredients

### Fats

**Butter**: Organic is better, since chemicals frequently get stored in the fat of animals. Use unsalted butter. The freshest cream goes into making unsalted butter, because salt acts as a preservative and can mask unpleasant flavors in the cream. Goat butter is easiest to digest, but some people find its flavor objectionable.

**Coconut oil:** Organic coconut oil is the best butter alternative if you are vegan or lactose intolerant. It is the least processed, can withstand heating, and the health benefits are compelling.

Coconut oil is nature's richest source of medium-chain fatty acids, which are easily absorbed and converted into energy. It is lower in calories than other fats and has been shown to stimulate metabolism and help with weight loss. Studies have found it free of trans fats and lower in cholesterol than other oils.[32] Be sure to look for raw, unrefined extra virgin or virgin coconut oil. Many markets carry it, or you can order it online. If replacing butter with coconut oil, use slightly less as it is more concentrated.

**Oil**: Mild flavored organic oils such as almond, sunflower, grapeseed or safflower may be used in the baked recipes.

I've included margarine as a recipe alternative, but I do not believe it is a healthy choice ingredient. I recommend replacing margarine with coconut oil in the recipes. We all know that traditional margarines contain trans fats, which contribute to heart disease. Even the 'natural' margarines, though free of trans fats and gluten, still contain soy or canola oils, which can be genetically modified or highly processed.

### Eggs and Egg Replacements

**Eggs**: Use large organic, free-range eggs.

**Ener G Egg Replacer™**: When the recipe calls for three or fewer eggs, egg replacement may be used. It works best if whisked in a small amount of recipe liquid before blending it in.

**Other egg replacements**: One egg in a recipe can be replaced with any of the following:

- ¼ cup mashed potato
- ¼ cup cooked pumpkin or winter squash
- ¼ cup mashed banana
- 1 tablespoon ground flax seed mixed in 3 tablespoons water
- 1 teaspoon ground chia seed mixed in 3 tablespoons water

### Salt

I recommend Real Salt™, sea salt, celtic salt or Himalayan crystal salt instead of common table salt. Natural salts are mineral-rich, flavorful and healthier than common table salt. Remember to add less salt than the recipes call for if you are using salted fats.

### Milk

Use one of the following: cow's milk, goat's milk, nut or seed milk, or coconut milk. Nut milks can be purchased, but read labels to be certain there is no sugar added. See the recipe on page 17 for making your own nut or seed milk using almonds, hazelnuts, hemp seeds, cashews, sunflower seeds, pecans, or walnuts. I prefer almond or cashew milk because of its mild flavor.

## Sugar's Bitter Side

The average American eats 160 pounds of sugar a year; that's more than two and a half pounds each week.[33] Processed foods flavored with sugar (especially high-fructose corn syrup) are contributing to our soaring rates of obesity and diabetes. Some estimates suggest that one quarter of the US population is at risk of developing diabetes. With so much sugar in the diet, it's not surprising that our bodies are reacting with record health problems.

Sugar, including refined flour, has been linked to a staggering number of health imbalances. Below I have listed some of them. Perhaps the most important single decision to protect health is to remove sugar from the diet. Substituting natural low-glycemic sweeteners for sugar may help alleviate these concerns and contribute to turning our current health crisis around.

## 12 Sugar-Related Health Problems

1. Obesity: Excess sugars in the body are stored as fat. [34]

2. Arthritis, stiffness and inflammation: Sugar, wheat, corn (high-fructose corn syrup), and dairy (lactose) are believed to cause inflammation in the body, leading to pain and stiffness. [35]

3. Blood sugar problems: Hypoglycemia, diabetes, and insulin resistance are epidemic in our society today. Some reports estimate that the rate of diabetes has increased seven hundred percent in the last fifty years. [36]

4. Cancer: New research has uncovered the link between sugar consumption and some cancers. [37]

5. Infections: Yeasts, fungus, parasites, and bacteria all love sweets and starches. [38] Symptoms of yeast (such as Candida) overgrowth may include: fatigue, lethargy, depression, irritability, headaches, problems concentrating, muscle weakness, recurrent vaginal and urinary tract infections, athlete's foot, jock itch, persistent heartburn, indigestion, constipation, swollen joints, nasal congestion and sore throat. [39]

6. Depression: Refined sugars can lead to mood swings, high and low blood sugar, and depression. [40]

7. Food allergies: Corn is a common allergen, and high-fructose corn syrup is a cheap sweetener used in most processed foods.

8. Cardiovascular disease: Studies have linked sugar consumption to vascular problems. [41] Sugar can produce a significant rise in total cholesterol, triglycerides and bad cholesterol and a decrease in good cholesterol. [42]

9. Osteoporosis: People with osteoporosis are advised to limit sugar consumption, as it depletes important minerals. [43]

10. ADHD and hyperactivity: Changing to a gluten-free and sugar-free diet has had profound effects on many with these problems. [44]

11. Tooth decay: We all know what refined sugars do to tooth enamel. Some of the sweeteners used in this book actually kill bacteria that cling to the teeth.

12. Autoimmune diseases: Sugar has been linked to arthritis and multiple sclerosis. [45] [46]

## Easy Steps for Getting Started

Making sugar-free, gluten-free desserts is a new skill that will delight you and support your health. Once you have some of the ingredients, you can start producing nourishing, delicious treats.

- Get familiar with recipe ingredients from the introduction.
- Choose one or two beginning recipes.
- Shop for your sweeteners or order them online.
- Get your recipe ingredients and equipment together.
- Buy ingredients to make your flour blend or purchase a commercial one.
- Start creating!

## Making the Recipes Work for You

I invite you to get to know these recipes, then make them your own. They have been well tested to be dependable, but you may want them more or less sweet, depending on your tastes; you may have ideas for ingredients that would add a unique flair. If you come up with a recipe you'd like to share, send it to **www.asweetlifewithoutsugar.com** and I'll test it to post on the site.

If you're used to eating wheat, give yourself some time to adjust to gluten-free grains, as their taste and texture are slightly different. The raw recipes and the various truffles and confections contain no grains.

See the shopping suggestions in the previous sections to begin stocking your kitchen. Parchment paper (unbleached is best) is handy for lining pans or to lay candies on. Read through several recipes you'd like to try and be sure you have appropriate pans and ingredients. Then push up your sleeves and have fun!

## Baking Tips

- Have all ingredients at room temperature.
- Position your rack in the center of the oven.
- Get an oven thermometer. Ovens vary a lot.
- Fill your measuring cup with flour, then drag the non-sharp edge of a knife across the top of the cup. Never pack or shake the flour down.
- Unbleached parchment paper is handy for lining cookie sheets.
- Be attentive: Baking times will vary depending on the size of the pan or the size of your baked goods.
- Keep wooden toothpicks on hand to test cakes when they are done baking.

## Joanie's Gluten-Free Flour Blend

This baking blend may be substituted in any recipe calling for unbleached white or wheat flour.

>    4 cups brown rice flour
>    1 cup quinoa flour
>    1 cup sorghum flour
>    ½ cup tapioca flour
>    4 teaspoons xanthan gum

1.  Whisk or sift the ingredients together several times and store in an airtight container, preferably in the refrigerator or freezer. If you can't find quinoa and sorghum flour, put in an equal amount of other gluten-free flours, such as buckwheat, amaranth, garbanzo, almond, teff, or millet. Corn starch or arrowroot can substitute for the tapioca flour. The xanthan gum helps to bind the gluten-free flours together when moistened.

## Making Nut or Seed Milk

Almonds or cashews have the mildest taste. It's best to soak the nuts for a few hours.

>    ½ cup nuts or seeds
>    2 cups water
>    Pinch stevia (optional)

1.  In a blender combine nuts, water & stevia.

2.  Cover and blend on high until smooth. You can use the milk as is or strain it through several layers of cheesecloth or a nut milk bag.

Milk will keep for several days in the refrigerator. For whiter milk, use blanched almonds. A quicker method is to blend 2 cups water with ¼ cup nut or seed butter.

# References

1. *Obesity Research* 10(6) (June 2002) 478-88.

2. Jeppesen, PB, et al. Department of Endocrinology and Metabolism, Aarhus University Hospital, Denmark; *Metabolism* (February 2000) 49(2):208-14.

3. Johnson, Dr. R. Elton, Jr; Stevioside, "Naturally!" A Special Presentation To The Calorie Control Council 23rd Annual Meeting Tucson, Arizona (November 4-7, 1990).

4. *Dr. Julian Whitaker's Health & Healing®*, (December 1994) Vol. 4, No12.

5. Bonvie, Bill, Bonvie, Linda, Gates, Donna; The Stevia Story: A tale of incredible sweetness & intrigue. © 2000 by Donna Gates.

6. Willet W, Manson J., Lu S.; Glycemic index, glycemic load and risk of type 2 diabetes. *American Journal of Clinical Nutrition.* (2002)76 (Supplement): 274S-80S.

7. Genta S, Cabrera W, Habib N, Pons J, Carillo IM, Grau A, Sánchez S.; *Clinical Nutrition.* Instituto Superior de Investigaciones Biológicas (INSIBIO), Consejo Nacional de Investigaciones Científicas y Técnicas (CONICET), Universidad Nacional de Tucumán (UNT), Chacabuco 461, 4000-San Miguel de Tucumán, Tucumán, Argentina. (2009 Feb 28).

8. IBID.

9. GRAS Notice 000297: Erythritol fatty acid esters www.accessdata.fda.gov/scripts/fcn/gras_notices/grn0297.pdf.

10. Bernt, W.O., Borzelleca, J.F., Flamm, G., Munto, I.C. Erythritol: A Review of Biological and Toxicological Studies. Regulatory Toxicology and Pharmacology 24 (1996) Article No. 0098: S191-S197.

11. A sweet problem: Princeton researchers find that high-fructose corn syrup prompts considerably more weight gain. Posted March 22, 2010 by Hilary Parker © 2010. The Trustees of Princeton University. Princeton, New Jersey 08544 USA.

12. Richard J. Johnson, MD.; The Sugar Fix: The high-fructose fallout that is making you fat and sick. © 2008 by Richard J Johnson with Timothy Gower: 55.

13. "US Patent 5846333–Method of producing fructose syrup from agave plants," Patent Storm.

14. Richard J. Johnson, MD.; The Sugar Fix: The high-fructose fallout that is making you fat and sick. © 2008 by Richard J. Johnson with Timothy Gower: 7.

15. IBID: 9,11.

16. IBID: 10-11,61-63.

17. American Journal of Clinical Nutrition, Vol. 76, No. 5 (November 2002)© 2002 American Society for Clinical Nutrition: 911-922.

18. A sweet problem: Princeton researchers find that high-fructose corn syrup prompts considerably more weight gain. Posted March 22, 2010 by Hilary Parker © 2010. The Trustees of Princeton University. Princeton, New Jersey 08544 USA.

19. Richard J. Johnson, MD.; The Sugar Fix: The high-fructose fallout that is making you fat and sick. © 2008 by Richard J. Johnson with Timothy Gower: 29-32.

20. IBID: 10-11.

21. IBID: 11.

22. IBID: 53-56.

23. IBID: 83-86.

24. IBID: 10-11,61-63.

25. IBID: 88-89,135.

26. Department of Health and Human Services; Report on All Adverse Reactions in the Adverse Reaction Monitoring System, (February 25 and 28, 1994).

27. http://www.mayoclinic.org/news2009-rst/5329.html.

28. Lewey, Dr. Scot; Gluten Sensitivity: A Gastroenterologist's Personal Journey Down the Gluten Rabbit Hole. Scot-Free Newsletter (01/30/2007).

29. Celiac Disease. Mayo Foundation for Medical Education and Research; ©2001-2010.

30. http://www.mayoclinic.org/news2009-rst/5329.html.

31. Dowd, B. and Smith, J. Walker; "Samuel Gee, Aretaeus, and the celiac affection." Abstract, British Medical Journal (1974, April 6) 2(5909): 45-47.

32. Fife, Bruce. The Coconut Oil Miracle. © 2004 by Bruce Fife, C.N., N.D.

33. Francis, Raymond. Never Be Sick Again. © 2002 Raymond Francis: 90.

34. Keen, H., et al. Nutrient Intake, Adiposity, and Diabetes. British Medical Journal (1989) 1:00 655-658.

35. Sutherland, Caroline. The Body Knows How to Stay Young. © 2007 – 2009 by Caroline Sutherland.

36. Reuters (October 30, 2008).

37. Quillin, Patrick; Cancer's Sweet Tooth. Nutrition Science News (April 2000) Rothkopf, M.. Nutrition. (July/Aug 1990)6(4).

38. Raymond Francis, Never Be Sick Again. © 2002 Raymond Francis: 92.

39. Crook, W. J.; The Yeast Connection. TN:  1984 by Professional Books.

40. Christensen, L.; The Role of Caffeine and Sugar in Depression. Nutrition Report (March 1991) 9(3): 17-24.

41. Howard, Barbara, PhD, Wylie-Rosett, Judith, RD, EdD; Sugar and Cardiovascular Disease: A Statement for Healthcare Professionals From the Committee on Nutrition of the Council on Nutrition, Physical Activity, and Metabolism of the American Heart Association.

42. Albrink, M. and Ullrich I. H.; Interaction of Dietary Sucrose and Fiber on Serum Lipids in Healthy Young Men Fed High Carbohydrate Diets. American Journal of Clinical Nutrition (1986) 43:419.

43. Tjäderhane, L. and Larmas, M.; A High Sucrose Diet Decreases the Mechanical Strength of Bones in Growing Rats. Journal of Nutrition (1998)128:1807, 1810.

44. Berdonces, J. L.; Attention Deficit and Infantile Hyperactivity. Pediatrics Research (1995) 38(4):539-542 Rev Enferm (Jan 2001) 4(1)11-4.

45. Darlington, L., Ramsey, N. W. and Mansfield, J. R.; Placebo Controlled, Blind Study of Dietary Manipulation Therapy in Rheumatoid Arthritis Lancet (Feb 1986) 8475(1):236,238.

46. Erlander, S.; The Cause and Cure of Multiple Sclerosis, The Disease to End Disease (Mar 3, 1979)1(3): 59,63.

# beginning recipes

This section includes
a wide variety of desserts.
Once you have your
ingredients, you're ready
to create, enjoy,
and thrive.

# Oatmeal Cookies

These satisfying cookies offer superior nutrition.
Goji berries (also called wolfberries) act as an antioxidant.
Flax seeds are rich in healthy fats.

2/3 cup butter, margarine or coconut oil, softened

2 eggs or egg replacement

½ cup grated apple

2 teaspoons vanilla extract

3 tablespoons yacon syrup

1½ cups gluten-free flour blend

1/8 -¼ teaspoon pure stevia powder

½ teaspoon baking soda

½ teaspoon baking powder

½ teaspoon salt

2 cups gluten-free rolled oats or quinoa flakes

½ cup raisins (optional)

½ cup chopped nuts

½ cup sunflower or pumpkin seeds

¼ cup ground flax seeds

½ cup goji berries

1. Preheat the oven to 350°.

2. Cream the butter, eggs, apple, vanilla and yacon.

3. Sift or whisk together the flour, stevia, baking soda, baking powder, and salt.

4. Combine the flour mixture with the ingredients from step 2.

5. Stir in the oats, raisins, nuts, seeds, and berries.

6. Drop by teaspoons onto a greased or lined baking sheet.

7. Bake for 12 to 15 minutes or until golden.

# Brownies With Mashed Yam

*These taste quite rich, with very little butter and no sugar.*
*Brownies usually depend on the sugar for that chewy texture,*
*but yam is a good substitute.*

4 tablespoons butter, margarine, or coconut oil

2/3 cup mashed cooked yam

1 egg or egg replacement

1 tablespoon vanilla extract

1/2 cup yacon syrup

2/3 cup unsweetened cocoa or carob powder

1/2 cup gluten-free flour or flour blend

1/4 teaspoon baking soda

1/8 - 1/4 teaspoon pure stevia powder

1/2 teaspoon salt

1. Preheat the oven to 325°.

2. Melt the butter, margarine or coconut oil over low heat.

3. In a mixing bowl or processor, beat the butter, yam, egg, vanilla, and yacon.

4. Whisk or sift several times the cocoa, flour, baking soda, stevia and salt.

5. Stir the flour mixture into the wet ingredients just enough to mix.

6. Pour the batter in a greased 8-inch square brownie pan.

7. Bake for 25 minutes or until barely firm but not hard.

8. Cool in the pan and cut. Makes 16 brownies.

# Jam Thumbprints

They look festive, and they are fast and easy to prepare in a food processor.
Instead of fruit spread, you can top each with a slivered almond or a pecan.

1 cup almonds, walnuts or pecans
½ cup rolled oats or quinoa flakes
½ cup shredded unsweetened coconut
1½ cup gluten-free flour blend
⅛ teaspoon pure stevia powder
½ teaspoon salt
½ teaspoon baking powder
½ cup butter or coconut oil
1 teaspoon vanilla
¼ cup yacon syrup
Unsweetened fruit spread

1. Preheat the oven to 350°.

2. In a food processor, with the "S" blade, grind the nuts until fine but not oily.

3. Add the oats or quinoa flakes, coconut, flour, stevia, salt and baking powder and pulse a few times.

4. Slice the butter into four chunks and add it, along with the vanilla and yacon. If using coconut oil, use 6 tablespoons.

5. Process until the dough starts to hold together.

6. Roll into balls, about 1 inch in diameter.

7. Place them on a greased or lined cookie sheet.

8. In the center of each ball make an indentation with your thumb.

9. Fill each with a spoonful of unsweetened fruit spread.

10. Bake until slightly brown, about 15 minutes.

# Upside Down Fruit Cobbler

*This recipe is easy and fun. The biscuit layer starts on the bottom and floats up through the fruit, to thicken it.*

**Biscuit layer**

1 cup gluten-free flour blend
1/8 teaspoon pure stevia powder
3 teaspoons baking powder
Pinch salt
1 cup milk (dairy, nut or coconut)

**Fruit layer**

2½ cups fruit (berries, cherries, sliced peaches or apples)
¼ cup yacon syrup
1/8 teaspoon pure stevia powder
2 tablespoons lemon juice
½ cup juice or water
2 tablespoons butter

**Biscuit layer**

1. Preheat the oven to 350°.

2. Whisk or sift together the flour, stevia, baking powder and salt.

3. Stir in the milk just enough to moisten the dry ingredients.

4. Pour the batter into a medium casserole or cake pan.

5. Spread the batter to fill the pan.

**Fruit layer**

1. Mix the fruit with the yacon, stevia, lemon juice and water or juice.

2. Spoon the fruit over the batter, spreading gently.

3. Cut the butter into small pieces and dot the cobbler.

4. Bake in the center of the oven for 1 hour or until the biscuit looks firm.

# Raw Chocolate Cheesecake

Dairy-free, creamy and bursting with flavor,
these raw cheesecakes are quick to make in a blender.

## Crust

½ cup pecans or walnuts, soaked 15 minutes
and drained
½ cup cacao powder
½ cup unsweetened fine-shred coconut
¼ teaspoon cinnamon (optional)
⅛ teaspoon stevia powder
2 tablespoons yacon syrup

## Filling

3 cups cashews
2 cups almond milk
¼ cup yacon syrup
¼ teaspoon stevia powder
1 tablespoon vanilla
½ cup cacao powder
1 tablespoon mesquite meal (optional)
¾ cup coconut butter

## Crust

1. Before starting the crust, soak the cashews in the almond milk for 1 hour. Don't drain. Save for the filling.

2. Meanwhile, combine crust ingredients in a processer and process until dough forms.

3. Spread the crust in the bottom of a 9-inch spring-form pan. Press firmly to form a crust on the bottom of the pan only.

## Filling

1. In a high-powered blender, combine the cashews soaked in almond milk, yacon, stevia, and vanilla. Blend on high until mixture is creamy.

2. Add the cacao, mesquite and coconut butter and blend again. Mixture will be thick.

3. Spread the filling evenly over the crust.

4. Freeze for 1-2 hours, then refrigerate until firm.

5. Remove ring and slice into 12 pieces.

# Raw Lemon Cheesecake

A perfect blend of sweet and tart.

**Crust**

¾ cup walnuts
¾ cup pecans

**Filling**

3 cups cashews, soaked 1 hour
Zest of 2 large lemons
1 cup lemon juice
1½ cups almond milk
⅓ cup yacon syrup (or 3 chopped dates)
¼ teaspoon pure stevia powder
¾ cup coconut butter

**Crust**

1. Soak the walnuts and pecans in 1 cup water for 15 minutes. Drain well.

2. Grind in a food processor or chop fine.

3. Spread the crust onto the bottom of a 9-inch spring-form pan.

**Filling**

1. Drain the cashews.

2. Zest the lemons then juice them.

3. In a strong blender, blend the cashews, lemon juice, almond milk, and yacon or dates until creamy.

4. Add the stevia, zest, and coconut butter, and blend well.

5. Pour the filling onto the crust and spread gently.

6. Freeze for 2 hours, then refrigerate for at least 2 hours before serving.

# Rich Apple Muffins

These are delicious as muffins, or they can become cupcakes
with one of the icings in the cake section.

1 cup buttermilk, yogurt or sour milk (see step 2)

1/3 cup butter, margarine, or coconut oil, melted

2 eggs or egg replacement

1/4 cup yacon syrup

2 teaspoons vanilla

1 apple, peeled and grated

2 cups gluten-free flour blend

1/8 teaspoon pure stevia powder

3/4 teaspoon baking soda

1/2 teaspoon salt

1 teaspoon cinnamon or apple pie spice

1/2 cup chopped nuts (optional)

1. Preheat the oven to 375°.

2. To make sour milk: Mix nut or dairy milk with 2 teaspoons apple cider vinegar.

3. Stir together the buttermilk, yogurt or sour milk, butter, eggs, yacon, vanilla and apple.

4. Sift or whisk together the flour, stevia, baking soda, salt and cinnamon.

5. Add the dry ingredients to the wet, stirring just enough to mix. Stir in nuts.

6. Grease or line muffin pans with muffin cups.

7. Fill each cup 2/3 full.

8. Bake 25 minutes or until the muffins feel firm to the touch but not hard.

9. Remove from oven and cool on wire racks.

# Chocolate Truffles with Cacao Nibs

Cacao is raw chocolate. It is filled with nutrients and acts
as an antioxidant. Coconut butter offers healthy fats.

¼ cup cacao nibs
½ cup coconut butter, softened
⅛ teaspoon pure stevia powder
3 tablespoons yacon syrup
2 teaspoons alcohol-free vanilla
¼ cup cacao (or cocoa) powder

1. Cacao nibs are quite hard; to soften them, stir in 1 tablespoon water and let them sit for a few minutes.

2. Soften the measured coconut butter by setting the measuring cup in a bowl of hot water for a few minutes.

3. Mix together the coconut butter, stevia, yacon syrup, and vanilla.

4. Stir in the cacao powder and the cacao nibs.

5. If the dough is too soft, refrigerate 5 minutes.

6. Form into balls. Makes 16 truffles.

For more candy see page 67.

# Carrot Cake

The perennial favorite made even healthier.

½ cup soft butter or coconut oil
  (or mild-flavored oil)
3 eggs or egg replacement
1½ tablespoons grated fresh ginger
  (or 1½ teaspoons dry)
2 teaspoons vanilla extract
⅓ cup yacon syrup
2 cups finely-grated or pureed carrots
2 cups gluten-free flour blend
2 teaspoons baking powder
1 teaspoon baking soda
⅛-¼ teaspoon pure stevia powder
3 teaspoons cinnamon
1 teaspoon salt
1 13-oz can unsweetened crushed pineapple
1 cup toasted walnuts or pecans, chopped

1. Preheat the oven to 350°.

2. In a large bowl combine the butter, eggs, ginger, vanilla, and yacon.

3. Beat with a mixer or heavy spoon until well blended.

4. Mix in the carrots.

5. Sift or whisk together the flour, baking powder, baking soda, stevia, cinnamon, and salt.

6. Add the flour mixture to the wet ingredients, stirring just enough to mix.

7. Fold in the pineapple and nuts.

8. Bake in a 9" by 13" pan for 40 minutes, or until a toothpick inserted comes out dry.

9. Let the cake cool before frosting with either of the following frostings.

## Vegan Coconut Frosting

1 13-oz can coconut milk
1 cup raw cashews
1/3 cup yacon syrup (or 3 chopped dates)
1/8 teaspoon pure stevia powder
1 tablespoon vanilla
Pinch salt
1/2 cup coconut butter

1. Soak the cashews in the coconut milk for 20 minutes.

2. Put all the ingredients into a blender, cover and blend until very smooth.

3. Pour the frosting into a bowl.

4. Refrigerate for at least 1 hour before frosting the cake.

## Lemon-Cream Cheese Frosting

1/8 - 1/4 teaspoon pure stevia powder
Juice of 1 large lemon
2 teaspoons lemon zest (more to taste)
2 8 oz packages whipped cream cheese or
    tofu cream cheese, softened
3 tablespoons yacon syrup (optional)

1. Zest the lemon before juicing.

2. Dissolve the stevia in the lemon juice.

3. With a mixer or heavy spoon, blend all ingredients until creamy.

4. Spread on the cooled cake.

# Chocolate Beet Cake

*The beet adds sweetness and fiber to replace what sugar would give to the recipe.*
*If you're hesitant about beets, don't worry—you can't taste them.*

1 medium beet, peeled and chopped (or canned)

2 cups water

½ cup butter, coconut oil, or margarine, softened

2 tablespoons vanilla extract

1 tablespoon apple cider vinegar

½-¾ cup yacon syrup

2 cups gluten-free flour blend

1¼ cups unsweetened cocoa or carob powder

2 teaspoons baking soda

1 teaspoon baking powder

1 teaspoon salt

½ teaspoon pure stevia powder

1. If using a raw beet, cook in water until it's tender. Drain and reserve the cooking water. Drain canned beets, reserving the water.

2. Measure the cooking (or canned) water, adding more if needed to equal 2 cups.

3. Puree the beet in the 2 cups of water. Set aside.

4. Preheat the oven to 350°.

5. In a large bowl, beat the butter, vanilla, vinegar, and yacon.

6. Beat in the pureed beet.

7. Sift or whisk together the flour, cocoa, baking soda, baking powder, salt and stevia several times.

8. Add the flour mixture to the wet ingredients and beat well by hand or with a mixer until fluffy.

9. Pour the batter into two greased 8-inch round cake pans, cupcake pans, or 9x13-inch rectangular pan.

10. Bake 30 minutes in the center of your oven or until a toothpick inserted in the center of the cake comes out dry. Cupcakes take 20 minutes.

11. Cool on racks until ready to frost.

## Buttercream Chocolate Frosting

1 cup milk (dairy, nut, or coconut)
½ cup butter, coconut oil or margarine
4 oz. unsweetened solid chocolate
2 teaspoons vanilla
⅛ teaspoon pure stevia powder
6 medjool dates, pitted and chopped fine

1. In a medium-sized saucepan, heat the milk.

2. Turn off the heat and add the butter, coconut oil or margarine

3. Break or chop the chocolate into pieces and add to the milk.

4. Stir until everything is melted.

5. Put this mixture into a blender along with the vanilla, stevia, and dates.

6. Blend until smooth and creamy.

7. Empty the frosting into a bowl. It will still be runny.

8. Refrigerate for about ½ hour or until frosting starts to set up. Frost your cake or cupcakes.

## Cream Cheese Frosting

5 cups whipped cream cheese
⅛-¼ teaspoon pure stevia powder
1 teaspoon vanilla
¼ cup yacon syrup

1. Stir or beat everything together with a spoon or mixer.

2. If you have an icing bag with decorator tips, it's fun to pipe this frosting onto cakes or cupcakes.

# Quinoa Breakfast Cake

This cake boasts a hefty amount of protein with the quinoa,
almond meal flour, eggs, and sunflower seeds.
In some markets, quinoa flakes can be found with the hot cereals.

1 ½ cups quinoa flakes

1 cup gluten-free flour blend

¾ cup almond meal flour (or coconut flour)

⅛ teaspoon pure stevia powder

2 teaspoons baking powder

½ teaspoon baking soda

½ teaspoon salt

1 teaspoon cinnamon

Pinch nutmeg

2 bananas, mashed

¼ cup soft butter, coconut oil or oil

2 eggs or egg replacement

2 teaspoons vanilla

¼ cup yacon syrup

½ cup lightly toasted sunflower seeds

⅓ cup raisins (optional)

1. Preheat the oven to 350°.

2. To make your own almond meal flour, grind blanched or plain almonds in a heavy blender or food processor until they are a fine meal.

3. Stir together the quinoa flakes, flour, almond meal, stevia, baking powder, baking soda, salt, cinnamon, and nutmeg.

4. In a separate bowl, beat the bananas, butter, eggs, vanilla, and yacon.

5. Stir the dry ingredients into the wet, just enough to moisten.

6. Stir in the sunflower seeds and raisins.

7. Grease or line a 9 x13-inch pan with parchment.

8. Spread the batter.

9. Bake 20-25 minutes.

10. Brush the cake with soft butter or coconut oil if desired.

# Apricot-Coconut Truffles

Sweet and tart—these truffles really pop.

½ cup coconut butter
12 dried Turkish apricots
2 tablespoons yacon syrup
1 teaspoon lemon zest
1 cup shredded, unsweetened coconut

1. Soften the coconut butter by placing the jar in a bowl of warm water.

2. Spoon out ½ cup.

3. Chop the apricots fine or cut them with scissors.

4. Stir together the coconut butter, apricots, yacon and zest.

5. Over low heat, lightly toast the shredded coconut in a dry pan until barely tan.

6. Roll the dough into ten one-inch balls.

7. Roll each ball in the toasted coconut.

8. Let the truffles set up until they are firm.

# cookies

Nothing says "home"
and "love" like a cookie.
These recipes promise to
nurture in all ways.

# Chewy Amaranth Cookies

These cookies are a great way to experience amaranth grain. Amaranth is a nutritional powerhouse: One half cup contains fourteen grams of usable protein, as well as vitamins and minerals. Look for it in the bulk section of your natural food store.

1 cup amaranth grain

2 cups water

½ cup butter, margarine, coconut oil or mild oil

2 teaspoons vanilla

1 cup applesauce (or cooked winter squash)

½ cup yacon syrup

1 beaten egg or egg replacement

1¾ cups gluten-free flour blend

2 teaspoons cinnamon

½ teaspoon nutmeg

¼ teaspoon cardamom (optional)

1 teaspoon baking soda

⅛ teaspoon pure stevia powder

½ teaspoon salt

1½ cups shredded unsweetened coconut

1. In a medium saucepan with tight-fitting lid, cook the amaranth in the water. When cooked, it will look like creamy hot cereal.

2. Preheat the oven to 350°.

3. Remove the amaranth from the heat and stir in the butter, vanilla, applesauce and yacon.

4. Empty the grain into a mixing bowl and cool.

5. Stir in the beaten egg.

6. Whisk or sift together several times the flour, cinnamon, nutmeg, cardamom, baking soda, stevia and salt.

7. Stir the dry ingredients into the amaranth.

8. Stir in the coconut.

9. Grease or line a baking sheet with parchment paper.

10. Drop by teaspoonfuls.

11. Bake for 10-12 minutes or until the cookies are slightly firm but still chewy.

# Carob Cookies with Orange

These will become a favorite, even for chocolate lovers.

2 cups almond flour (ground almonds)
½ cup + 2 tablespoons carob powder
1 teaspoon baking soda
¼ teaspoon salt
½ teaspoon xanthan gum (optional)
⅛ teaspoon pure stevia powder
Zest of 1 orange
½ cup soft butter, coconut butter or margarine
⅓ cup yacon syrup
2 teaspoons vanilla

1. Preheat the oven to 350°.

2. In a bowl, whisk together the flour, carob powder, baking soda, salt, xanthan gum, stevia, and orange zest.

3. In a separate bowl, beat together the butter, yacon syrup and vanilla.

4. Stir the dry ingredients into the wet ones, mixing well.

5. Roll the dough into 1-inch balls and place on a lined or ungreased baking sheet.

6. Flatten each ball slightly.

7. Bake 10-12 minutes. Cookies will be soft until they cool.

# Low-Fat Chocolate Chews

*Cannellini beans and cacao nibs give these cookies lots of richness with very little fat. Low-fat and no sugar? Pass the cookies, please!*

1 15 oz. can cannellini beans, drained
¼ cup yacon syrup
1 teaspoon vanilla
¼ cup butter, melted
½ cup erythritol
¼ teaspoon pure stevia powder
½ teaspoon salt
½ teaspoon baking soda
½ cup unsweetened cocoa powder
½ cup gluten-free flour blend
2 egg whites
½ cup cacao nibs

1. Preheat the oven to 350°.
2. In a processor, blend the beans, yacon, vanilla, and butter.
3. Add the erythritol, stevia, salt, baking soda, cocoa, and flour blend.
4. Pulse a few times to mix.
5. In a large bowl, beat the egg whites to soft peaks.
6. Carefully fold in the chocolate mixture and cacao nibs.
7. Grease or line a baking sheet.
8. Drop the cookies by teaspoons, leaving space between.
9. Spread each cookie out slightly.
10. Bake 10 to 13 minutes.

# Brownies

Getting the right texture without sugar or gluten was a challenge,
but I know you'll like this brownie.

6 oz. solid unsweetened chocolate

½ cup butter, coconut oil or margarine

¼ cup gluten-free flour blend

¼ cup unsweetened cocoa powder

¼ teaspoon pure stevia powder

½ teaspoon salt

¼ teaspoon baking soda

2 large eggs or egg replacement

½ cup yacon syrup

1 tablespoon vanilla

¼ cup erythritol

1 cup almond meal flour (finely-ground almonds)

½ cup chopped nuts (optional)

1. Preheat the oven to 325°.

2. Break up or chop the chocolate coarsely.

3. In a small heavy saucepan or double boiler, heat the butter and chocolate over very low heat until melted. Let cool slightly.

4. Meanwhile, whisk or sift together the flour blend, cocoa, stevia, salt, and baking soda. Set aside.

5. In a mixing bowl, beat the eggs until frothy. Continue beating while slowly adding the chocolate mixture.

6. Beat in the yacon, vanilla, and erythritol.

7. Stir in the flour mixture.

8. Stir in the ground almonds. Batter will be thick.

9. Spread the batter evenly in a greased 8x8 inch pan.

10. If using nuts, sprinkle on top and press slightly into the batter.

11. Bake for 30 minutes or until just firm. Don't bake too long, as the brownies will be tough, but test with a toothpick to be sure they are cooked through.

12. Cool and cut. Makes 16 small brownies.

# Walnut-Rosemary Biscotti

I adore biscotti! Try these with sliced tomatoes and goat cheese.

½ cup butter, coconut oil or margarine, softened

2 tablespoons lemon zest

2 eggs

3 tablespoons lemon juice

2 tablespoons + 1 teaspoon rosemary, crushed

3½ cups gluten-free flour blend

1 teaspoon salt

⅛ teaspoon pure stevia powder

1½ teaspoons baking powder

½ teaspoon baking soda

½ cup erythritol

3 cups walnuts, chopped fine

1. Preheat the oven to 325°.

2. Beat the butter, lemon zest, eggs, lemon juice and rosemary.

3. Sift or whisk together the flour, salt, stevia, baking powder, baking soda, and erythritol.

4. Stir the dry ingredients into the wet, mixing well.

5. Stir in the walnuts.

6. On a greased or lined baking sheet, shape the dough into a loaf, 3 inches wide.

7. Bake 35-40 minutes or until slightly brown.

8. Cool slightly, then transfer loaf to a cutting surface.

9. Reduce oven heat to 300°.

10. Cut the loaf into ½-inch slices.

11. Stand the slices up on the baking sheet with space between.

12. Bake another 40 minutes or until the biscotti are dry and crisp.

13. Cool and store in airtight containers or freeze.

# Chocolate Biscotti

Carob powder can replace the cocoa in this recipe.

½ cup soft butter, coconut oil, margarine, or oil

3 eggs

1 tablespoon vanilla

½ cup yacon syrup

2¼ cups gluten-free flour blend

1½ teaspoons baking powder

¾ teaspoon baking soda

½ teaspoon salt

⅔ cup cocoa powder

1½ teaspoons espresso powder (optional)

1 cup almond flour (ground almonds)

½ cup chopped walnuts (or other nuts)

½ cup cacao nibs (optional)

1. Preheat the oven to 350°.

2. Cream together the butter, eggs, vanilla, and yacon.

3. Sift or whisk together the flour, baking powder, baking soda, salt, cocoa, and espresso powder.

4. Stir the dry ingredients into the wet, mixing well.

5. Stir in the almond flour, walnuts and cacao nibs.

6. On a greased or lined baking sheet, form the dough into a loaf, 3 inches wide and the length of the sheet. Oil or wet your hands to make this easier.

7. Bake for 35 minutes or until the loaf is firm.

8. Remove from the oven and cool slightly.

9. Transfer the loaf to a cutting surface.

10. Lower the oven temperature to 275°.

11. Cut the loaf into ½-inch slices.

12. Stand the slices up on the baking sheet with space between.

13. Bake another 45 minutes or 1 hour, until the biscotti are crisp.

# Hazelnut Biscotti

These are so fabulous with a cup of hot tea.
Wrap them in cellophane and tie with a pretty bow for gifting.

½ cup soft butter, coconut oil or margarine

3 eggs

1 tablespoon vanilla

¼ cup yacon syrup

2½ cups gluten-free flour blend

1½ teaspoons baking powder

¾ teaspoon baking soda

½ teaspoon salt

1½ tablespoons anise seeds, crushed

⅛ teaspoon pure stevia powder

½ cup erythritol

1 cup toasted hazelnuts, finely chopped

1. Preheat the oven to 350°.

2. Beat the butter, eggs, vanilla, and yacon.

3. Whisk together the flour, baking powder, baking soda, salt, anise, stevia, and erythritol.

4. Stir the dry ingredients into the wet, mixing well.

5. Stir in the hazelnuts. Dough will be thick.

6. On a greased or lined baking sheet, form the dough into a loaf, 3 inches wide and the length of the pan. Wet or oil your hands to make this easier.

7. Bake 30 minutes or until slightly brown.

8. Remove the loaf and lower the oven temperature to 275°.

9. Cool the loaf slightly, then move it to a cutting surface.

10. Cut the loaf into ½-inch slices.

11. Stand the slices up on the baking sheet with space between.

12. Bake another 45 minutes or longer, until they are dry and crisp.

13. Cool thoroughly and store in airtight containers.

# Buckwheat Chocolate-Chunk Cookies

The buckwheat gives a wonderful flavor and chewy texture.
Make the chocolate chunks first, as they take some time to set up.

## Chocolate chunks

4 ounces unsweetened solid chocolate

1/8 teaspoon pure stevia powder

1 tablespoon yacon syrup

1 teaspoon liquid lecithin (optional)

## Cookies

2 cups almond flour (ground almonds)

3/4 cup buckwheat flour

1/4 cup gluten-free flour blend

1/4 teaspoon salt

1 teaspoon baking soda

1/8 teaspoon pure stevia powder

1/2 cup erythritol

1/2 cup softened butter, margarine, or coconut oil

1/4 cup yacon syrup

2 teaspoons vanilla

3/4 cup chocolate chunks

1/2 cup toasted walnuts or pecans, chopped

## Chocolate chunks

1. Melt the chocolate slowly over low heat.

2. Stir in the stevia, yacon syrup, and lecithin.

3. Pour chocolate onto a piece of waxed paper or parchment. Refrigerate to cool faster.

4. When firm, cut into 1/8-inch squares.

## Cookies

1. Preheat the oven to 350°.

2. In a bowl, whisk together the three flours, salt, baking soda, stevia and erythritol.

3. In a separate bowl, beat together the butter, yacon, and vanilla.

4. Stir the dry ingredients into the wet ones, mixing well.

5. Stir in the chocolate chunks and nuts.

6. Drop by teaspoons onto an ungreased or lined cookie sheet. Flatten slightly.

7. Bake 10-12 minutes.

# Ginger Snaps

Hold onto your socks! These really snap with ginger.

2 cups almond flour (ground almonds)
½ cup gluten-free flour blend
¼ teaspoon salt
1 teaspoon baking soda
⅛ teaspoon pure stevia powder
¼ cup erythritol
2 tablespoons ground ginger
1 teaspoon cinnamon
¼ teaspoon nutmeg
¼ teaspoon cloves
6 tablespoons butter, melted
¼ cup yacon syrup

1. Preheat the oven to 350°.
2. In a medium bowl, whisk together the flours, salt, baking soda, stevia, erythritol, and spices.
3. Stir the yacon syrup into the melted butter. Cool slightly.
4. Combine all ingredients.
5. Grease or line 2 cookie sheets.
6. Form dough into 1-inch balls.
7. Arrange the cookies on a greased or lined baking sheet. Flatten slightly.
8. Bake 15 minutes or until slightly brown.
9. Cookies will get crisp as they cool.

# Nut Butter Cookies

These familiar cookies can be made with peanut, almond, cashew, or sunflower seed butter.

¼ cup butter, coconut oil or margarine

1 cup nut butter

¼ cup yacon syrup

1 egg

2 teaspoons vanilla

1 ½ cup gluten-free flour blend

2 tablespoons erythritol

⅛ teaspoon pure stevia powder

½ teaspoon baking soda

½ teaspoon salt

1. Preheat the oven to 350°.

2. Melt the butter, coconut oil or margarine on low heat.

3. In a medium-sized bowl, combine the nut butter, butter, yacon, egg, and vanilla.

4. In a separate bowl, whisk together the flour, erythritol, stevia, baking soda, and salt.

5. Stir the flour mixture into the butter mixture.

6. Roll into balls, 1 inch in diameter.

7. Lay each ball on an ungreased or parchment-lined baking sheet.

8. Press each ball slightly with the tines of a fork in a crisscross pattern.

9. Bake 12-15 minutes.

# Gingerbread Cookies

These are fun to make at holiday time or anytime a gingerbread man or woman will lift your spirits. Dough squeezed through a clean garlic press makes great hair!

½ cup butter, margarine or coconut oil, softened

½ cup yacon syrup

1 egg or egg replacement

1 tablespoon apple cider vinegar

3 cups gluten-free flour blend

⅛ -¼ teaspoon pure stevia powder

1 teaspoon baking soda

4 teaspoons ground ginger

1½ teaspoons cinnamon

¼ teaspoon cloves

½ teaspoon nutmeg

½ teaspoon ground black pepper (optional)

1. Preheat the oven to 350°.

2. In a large bowl cream the butter, yacon, egg and vinegar.

3. Whisk or sift together the flour, stevia, baking soda, and spices.

4. Add the dry ingredients to the wet, mixing with a heavy spoon. The dough should be stiff.

5. Knead it a little in the bowl or on your work surface.

6. With a rolling pin, on a floured surface, roll the dough to ¼-inch thickness.

7. Cut into shapes with cookie cutters or a knife.

8. Grease or line several baking sheets.

9. Arrange the cookies with a little space between.

10. If you make different sized cookies, put them on different pans so the smaller ones don't burn.

11. Bake 10-15 minutes, depending on the size of your cookies and if you like them chewy or crunchy.

Gingerbread Cookies
*page 48*

Raw Key Lime Pie
with Meringue

*page 102*

Cacao-Goji Truffles
with Maca and Middle-
Eastern Truffles
*pages 68 & 69*

Coconut Cupcakes
*page 88*

Upside Down
Fruit Cobbler
*page 25*

Carob Cookies
with Orange
*page 39*

Carrot Cake

*page 30*

Raw Pumpkin Pie

*page 105*

Dipped Truffles
*page 74-77*

Trifle
*page 86*

Brownies
*page 41*

Stuffed Dates

*page 71*

Dehydrated Cranberry
Biscotti
*page 108*

Lemon Bars with
Ginger Crust

*page 65*

# Lemon Bars With Ginger Crust

These bars have a lot of zing.

## Crust

2 cups almond flour (ground almonds)
½ cup gluten-free flour blend
¼ teaspoon salt
1 teaspoon baking soda
⅛ teaspoon pure stevia powder
¼ cup erythritol
2 tablespoons ground ginger
6 tablespoons butter or coconut oil, melted
¼ cup yacon syrup

## Lemon Curd

½ cup erythritol
½ teaspoon pure stevia powder
Pinch salt
1 tablespoon lemon zest
⅔ cup lemon juice
⅓ cup orange juice
½ cup butter
4 eggs

## Crust

1. Preheat the oven to 350°.

2. In a medium-sized bowl, stir together the two flours, salt, baking soda, stevia, erythritol and ginger.

3. Stir together the butter and yacon.

4. Mix the butter into the flour mixture.

5. Pat out into an 8"x8" square pan.

6. Bake 12 minutes.

## Lemon Curd

1. Meanwhile, in a medium saucepan, stir together the erythritol, stevia, and salt.

2. Add the lemon zest, lemon juice, and orange juice and heat on medium to a simmer.

3. Cut the butter into 4 pieces and stir into the lemon juice.

4. In a medium-sized bowl, beat the eggs.

5. Slowly pour in the lemon juice, beating as you pour.

6. Pour the curd back into the pan and continue to cook, beating constantly, until it starts to thicken.

7. Slowly pour the lemon curd onto the base and return it to the oven for 15 minutes. Cool and cut into 16 bars.

# confections

It's not difficult to make
candies that look elegant
in their pleated paper cups.
Many of them are also
packed with nutrition.

# Cacao-Goji Truffles with Maca

These truffles seem to please everyone.
They taste fabulous and offer lots of nutrition.

¼ cup cacao nibs
¼ cup goji berries
3 tablespoons yacon syrup
2 teaspoons alcohol-free vanilla extract
1 cup nut butter (I use almond)
Pinch pure stevia powder
Pinch salt
1 tablespoon maca powder
1 cup shredded coconut, ground almonds or
    hemp seed for rolling the truffles

See page 98 to learn about maca.

1. If you want your truffles less chewy, soak the goji berries and cacao nibs in 2 tablespoons of water for 30-60 minutes.

2. In a medium-sized mixing bowl, stir together the yacon syrup, vanilla, and nut butter.

3. Stir in the stevia and salt.

4. Stir in the maca.

5. Stir in the cacao and goji berries.

6. Fill a small bowl with shredded coconut, ground almonds, or hemp seeds.

7. Scoop out a teaspoon of dough and roll it in your hands to form a ball.

8. Roll each of the balls in any of the coatings.

9. Roll in your hands again to press the coating into the ball.

10. Put each truffle into a candy cup or onto a serving plate or container. Makes 16.

# Middle-Eastern Truffles

Reminiscent of baklava, this dessert has far less fat and no wheat.

½ cup sesame tahini
¼ cup yacon syrup
Pinch salt
Pinch pure stevia powder
½ teaspoon orange zest or orange extract
½ cup fine-shred unsweetened coconut
1 cup finely chopped walnuts

1. In a small bowl, stir together the tahini, yacon, salt, stevia, zest and coconut.
2. Let the dough sit for a couple hours to firm up.
3. Fill a small bowl with the chopped walnuts.
4. Lift out a teaspoon of dough and roll it gently in your hands.
5. Roll it in the walnuts, pressing them lightly into the truffle.
6. Place the finished truffle into a candy cup.
7. Continue with the rest of the dough. Makes 16 truffles.
8. Refrigerate or freeze for storage.

# Carob-Cherry Confections

The almond accents the carob and cherries perfectly in this recipe.

1 cup dried cherries (unsweetened)
½ cup nut butter
1 teaspoon vanilla
⅛ teaspoon almond extract
2 tablespoons yacon syrup
Pinch pure stevia powder
Pinch salt
½ cup carob powder

1. If the cherries are quite dry, soak them in ½ cup water for 20 minutes or until they plump a bit. Drain them well, reserving the water, in case you need it later.

2. Stir together the nut butter, vanilla, almond extract and yacon.

3. Add the pure stevia powder and salt, stirring well to mix.

4. Stir in the carob powder.

5. Stir in the cherries.

6. If the dough is too thin, add a little more carob; if it's too thick, add a little soaking water or almond milk.

7. Form the dough into balls.

8. Serve in paper candy cups. Refrigerate or freeze for storage.

9. Substitute other dried fruits, if you prefer.

# Stuffed Dates

Medjool are considered the king of dates.
Middle Eastern markets often carry rose water.

12 medjool dates
Rose water
½ cup goat chevre (substitute almond butter,
   tahini or coconut butter, softened)
1 tablespoon culinary lavender blossoms

1. Cut a slit in the side of each date and remove the pit.

2. Mix equal parts of rose water with plain water.

3. Use a small spray bottle to spray the dates or dip your fingers and rub them on the dates. Go easy, as the rose water can be strong.

4. Open each date and fill with chevre.

5. Arrange the dates on a serving platter and crumble some lavender blossoms over them. Again go easy, as the taste is strong.

6. If you have some small edible flowers, like Johnny-jump-ups (Violas) or rose petals, sprinkle them around the plate. Life is divine!

Once you have your ingredients, this easy recipe will remind you that life is full of flowers!

# Lavender-Infused Fig Squares

Look for culinary lavender to avoid bitterness.

1 cup water
2 teaspoons dried lavender or a few sprigs fresh
8 dried black mission figs
Pinch pure stevia powder
4 tablespoons unsalted butter
1 cup carob powder
½ teaspoon fresh lavender blossoms
    (optional for garnish)

A few drops of Young Living™ lavender oil may be added to the water, instead of making tea. Young Living™ products are the purest I have found.

1. In a small covered saucepan bring the water to a simmer.
2. Turn off the heat and sprinkle in the dried or fresh lavender.
3. Cover and steep for at least 20 minutes. Strain into a bowl.
4. Meanwhile chop the figs fine.
5. Add the chopped figs, stevia, and butter to the warm lavender tea. Infuse in the tea for at least 2 hours or overnight.
6. Stir in the carob powder. The dough will set up as it cools, but if the mixture is too wet, add more carob powder.
7. On waxed paper or parchment, pat the dough out to a square, about 6 inches on a side.
8. If using the garnish, sprinkle lightly with tiny lavender blossoms, pressing them gently into the dough.
9. Cool the dough in the refrigerator until it's firm, about 2 hours.
10. Cut into small squares and serve.

# Hazelnut Truffles

*Chocolate and hazelnut are one of my favorite combinations.*

½ cup nut or coconut butter
2 teaspoons vanilla
¼ cup yacon syrup
Pinch stevia
⅓ cup cocoa powder
1 cup hazelnuts, ground fine

1. If you are using coconut butter, measure it and set the measuring cup into a bowl of warm water to soften it.

2. Stir together the nut or coconut butter, vanilla and yacon.

3. Stir in the stevia.

4. Stir in the cocoa.

5. Form the dough into bite-sized balls.

6. Roll each ball in the ground nuts.

# Carob-Fruit Chews

*Try different combinations of fruit and nuts. I like apricots or cherries and pecans. Be sure your dried fruit has no added sugar.*

⅓ cup carob powder
1 cup nut butter (almond, peanut, cashew)
2 tablespoons yacon syrup
1 teaspoon cinnamon (optional)
2 teaspoons alcohol-free vanilla
½ cup mixed dried fruit, chopped
½ cup chopped nuts
½ cup ground nuts or shredded coconut (optional)

1. In a mixing bowl combine the carob, nut butter, yacon syrup, cinnamon, and vanilla.

2. Stir in the fruit and nuts.

3. Form into balls with your fingers.

4. Balls can be rolled in ground nuts or coconut.

# Coconut Dipped Truffles

For many years I made traditional dipped truffles for family, friends, and as a business. It's been fun to explore more nourishing sugar–free variations of these ultimate confections. They aren't difficult to make and guaranteed to dazzle.

## Centers

½ cup coconut milk (canned or fresh)
½ cup coconut butter
4 tablespoons unsalted butter (for dairy-free, substitute coconut butter)
2 tablespoons yacon syrup or erythritol
Pinch pure stevia powder
½ cup unsweetened fine-shred coconut
¼ cup shredded or flaked coconut for garnish

## Dipping chocolate

8 oz. unsweetened solid chocolate
1 teaspoon liquid lecithin (optional)
1/8-1/4 teaspoon pure stevia powder
1 tablespoon yacon syrup

1. In a small saucepan, bring the coconut milk to a simmer.

2. Turn off the heat and add everything except the garnish coconut, stirring well to mix.

3. Pour the mixture into a bowl and refrigerate until firm.

4. With a teaspoon, scoop out a piece and form it into a grape-sized ball using your fingertips. Set it on a plate.

5. Continue with the remaining filling.

6. Return the centers to the refrigerator or freezer until they are very firm.

7. Follow the directions for dipping.

## To dip the truffles

1. Make a mini-double boiler, using a small bowl that sits snuggly on a saucepan with 1-2 inches of water.

2. Turn off the heat before it boils.

3. Break or chop the chocolate into small chunks.

4. Begin melting the chocolate in the bowl of the double boiler.

5. Stir with a wooden chopstick or small spatula while it melts. (This will take some time.)

6. When the chocolate is melted, stir in the other ingredients. Reheat water if necessary.

7. Drop a center into the chocolate.

8. Turn the center over to coat with chocolate. (I use a small fork and the chopstick.)

9. When it's coated, lift with the fork, scraping excess chocolate from the bottom of the fork.

10. Turn the center over and lay it on a piece of waxed or parchment paper. You need to get your truffle off of your fork before the tines dig into the candy.

11. If any places aren't covered with the chocolate, rub with the fork or chopstick to fill them.

12. If you want to garnish your truffles, when each truffle goes onto the waxed paper, sprinkle it with a pinch of coconut.

13. Repeat with the remaining centers, stirring the chocolate frequently. When the chocolate is completely set up, you can serve the truffles or store them in a container in the refrigerator or freezer.

A tiny crock-pot called "Little Dipper"™ melts chocolate at low temperatures.

# Hazelnut Dipped Truffles

These make lovely gifts at holiday time.

## Centers

½ cup coconut milk or heavy cream
1/8 teaspoon pure stevia powder
¼ cup yacon syrup
3 tablespoons unsalted butter or coconut oil
4 oz. unsweetened solid chocolate
¾ cup toasted hazelnuts, chopped fine
1 tablespoon cocoa or carob powder
     (optional for garnish)

## Dipping chocolate

8 oz. unsweetened solid chocolate
1 teaspoon liquid lecithin (optional)
1/8 teaspoon pure stevia powder
1 tablespoon yacon syrup

1. In a small heavy saucepan, heat the coconut milk or cream to a simmer.

2. Turn off the heat and stir in the stevia, yacon, butter, and chocolate.

3. Continue stirring until the mixture looks smooth.

4. Empty the chocolate mixture into a bowl.

5. Stir in the nuts.

6. Cover and refrigerate until firm.

7. With a teaspoon, scoop some of the mixture and roll it in your hands or press it with your fingers into a ball. It should be grape-sized or a little larger. If the mixture is too firm to roll, let it sit out of the refrigerator for awhile.

8. Follow the instructions on page 75 for preparing the coating chocolate and dipping.

9. While the chocolate coating is still soft, garnish with a little unsweetened cocoa or carob powder.

10. When the chocolate is completely set up, the truffles can go into candy cups.

11. For storage, refrigerate or freeze in airtight containers.

# Raspberry Dipped Truffles

Raspberries and chocolate—a sublime combination!

## Centers

½ cup heavy cream or coconut milk
5 tablespoons unsalted butter, cubed
⅛ teaspoon pure stevia powder
¼ cup coconut butter or cocoa butter
¾ cup fruit-sweetened raspberry preserves

## Dipping chocolate

8 oz. unsweetened solid chocolate
1 teaspoon liquid lecithin (optional)
⅛ teaspoon pure stevia powder
1-2 tablespoons yacon syrup

1. In a small saucepan, gently heat the cream to a simmer.

2. Turn off the heat.

3. Stir in the butter, stevia and coconut or cocoa butter.

4. Keep stirring until everything is melted and combined.

5. Stir in the preserves, blending well.

6. Empty filling into a bowl and refrigerate several hours or overnight.

7. Scoop out a teaspoon of filling and form into a ball with your fingertips. Place on a plate or tray.

8. Freeze the centers until firm, about an hour.

9. Follow instructions on page 75 for dipping centers.

# cakes, pies & tarts

These times call for
creating new classics,
pleasing to our tastes and
to our bodies.

# Upside Down Salad Cake

*Though the name sounds strange, it's a great way to eat your veggies.*

## Topping

6 tablespoons butter, coconut butter or margarine

1 tablespoon yacon syrup

½ tablespoon cornstarch, tapioca flour,
    or arrowroot

⅛ teaspoon pure stevia powder

1 teaspoon lemon zest

1½ cups fresh or frozen blueberries, thawed

(Substitute other fruits such as apples,
    pineapple, or cherries.)

## Cake

1 each: small carrot, ½ small beet, small
    wedge cabbage, small apple

1 cup milk (nut, coconut, or dairy)

2 eggs or egg replacement

2 teaspoons vanilla

1¾ cups gluten-free flour blend

1 teaspoon cinnamon

½ teaspoon baking soda

2 teaspoons baking powder

½ teaspoon salt

⅛-¼ teaspoon pure stevia powder

## Topping

1. Heat the butter and yacon in a small saucepan. Pour into an 8" or 9" cake pan.

2. In a medium sized bowl, stir together the cornstarch, stevia and zest. Add the blueberries stirring to coat.

3. Spread into cake pan.

## Cake

1. Preheat the oven to 350°.

2. Grate the carrot, beet, cabbage, and apple or pulse in a food processor until fine, but not mushy.

3. Beat the milk, eggs, and vanilla. Stir in the grated vegetables.

4. In a separate bowl, sift or whisk together the flour, cinnamon, baking soda, baking powder, salt and stevia.

5. Stir the dry ingredients into the wet ones.

6. Spread the cake batter over the topping.

7. Bake 40 minutes or until a tester comes out dry.

8. Remove from the oven, cover with a serving plate, and flip the cake over. Wait 5 minutes before lifting off the cake pan.

# Baked Pumpkin Pie

Butternut squash makes the sweetest pie. Bake up a big one for dinner
and use the leftovers. This pie is even better the second day.

## Crust

1 cup ground pecans or walnuts
1 cup gluten-free flour blend
Pinch pure stevia powder
½ teaspoon salt
½ cup butter, margarine or coconut oil
⅓ cup ice water

## Filling

1½ cups cooked pumpkin or squash
1½ cups milk (dairy, nut or coconut)
2 large eggs
½ cup yacon syrup (or 8 soaked dates)
⅛-¼ teaspoon pure stevia powder
2 teaspoons cinnamon
½ teaspoon each nutmeg and ginger
⅛ teaspoon cloves
Pinch salt
1 tablespoon cornstarch or arrowroot

## Crust

1. In a food processor or by hand, mix the nuts, flour, stevia and salt.

2. Cut in the butter to coarse crumbs.

3. Add just enough ice water to barely start to hold the dough together. (Less water means a flakier crust.)

4. Press the crust into a pie pan, working it up the sides.

## Filling

1. Preheat the oven to 350°.

2. Mix all filling ingredients in a blender or food processor until smooth.

3. Pour filling into the prepared crust.

4. Bake for about 40 minutes or until a knife inserted in the center comes out clean.

# Fruitcake

This is a healthier alternative to the classic fruitcake, which contains sulphured and candied dried fruits. Unsulphured fruits are usually darker in color and less plump.

## Preparing the Fruit

1 cup raisins (I like golden)

½ cup each: dried cherries, apricots, pineapple, dates, figs, cranberries or currants

1 cup fruit juice, rum, or water

## Cake

½ cup butter, margarine or coconut oil, softened

3 large eggs

Zest of 1 lemon

Zest of 1 orange

1 tablespoon vanilla

½ cup yacon syrup

1 cup gluten-free flour blend

½ teaspoon salt

½ teaspoon allspice

½ teaspoon ground ginger

⅛ teaspoon pure stevia powder

2 teaspoons baking powder

1 ½ cups lightly toasted pecans, walnuts or mixed nuts, chopped

## Fruit

1. With scissors or a knife, cut the larger fruits into small but recognizable pieces.

2. In a covered bowl, soak the fruit in the liquid overnight.

3. Orange, pomegranate, or other fruit juices work well, or use water with rum flavoring or vanilla extract.

## Cake

1. Preheat the oven to 275°.

2. Cream together the butter and eggs.

3. Beat in the zests, vanilla, and yacon.

4. Whisk or sift together several times the flour blend, salt, allspice, ginger, stevia, and baking powder.

5. Beat the creamed ingredients with the dry ingredients.

6. Stir in the fruits and nuts.

7. Spread the batter into two greased loaf pans.

8. Bake 1 hour or until a toothpick inserted into the middle comes out dry.

9. Cooled loaves may be brushed with brandy.

# Lemon-Poppy Seed Cake

Perfect for your next tea party.

¾ cup butter, coconut oil, margarine, or mild oil

⅓-½ cup erythritol or yacon syrup

½ cup almond meal (finely ground almonds)

4 eggs

1 teaspoon vanilla

1¼ cups gluten-free flour blend

2 teaspoons baking powder

½ teaspoon salt

¼ teaspoon pure stevia powder

½ cup milk (dairy, nut, coconut)

2 tablespoons lemon zest

3 tablespoons poppy seeds

1. Preheat the oven to 350°.

2. Be sure all ingredients are at room temperature.

3. Cream the butter with the erythritol or yacon syrup and the almonds.

4. Beat in the eggs, one at a time.

5. Continue beating until mixture loses its gloss and is fluffy. Beat in the vanilla.

6. Sift or whisk together the flour, baking powder, salt, and stevia.

7. On low speed, beat in ⅓ of the milk.

8. Beat in ⅓ of the flour mixture.

9. Continue 2 more times, ending with the dry ingredients.

10. Beat in the zest and poppy seeds.

11. Grease or line a loaf pan with parchment or use an 8" square or bundt pan. Spread the batter evenly.

12. Bake 40-60 minutes or until a tester comes out dry.

# Sponge Cake

*This fat–free cake is wonderful with fresh fruit or in Trifle.*
*It's light and delicate, so it pairs well with many toppings.*

5 eggs, separated
¼ teaspoon salt, divided
½ cup gluten-free flour blend
½ cup tapioca flour or cornstarch
¼ teaspoon pure stevia powder
1 teaspoon cream of tartar
½ cup erythritol or yacon syrup
½ cup almond meal
1 tablespoon orange zest
1 teaspoon vanilla

1. Preheat the oven to 350°.

2. Separate the egg whites and yolks into two medium-sized bowls.

3. Add half of the salt to the whites and half to the yolks.

4. Sift or whisk together the flours and stevia. Set aside.

5. Beat the egg whites until foamy.

6. Add the cream of tartar and beat to stiff peaks.

7. Beat the yolks with the erythritol or yacon, almond meal, zest and vanilla until thick and lemon-colored.

8. Gently fold the yolk mixture into the whites.

9. Gently fold in the flour mixture, a third at a time.

10. Grease a 9" square pan and dust it with flour or line with parchment paper.

11. Spread the batter evenly in the pan.

12. Bake for 35-40 minutes, or until a toothpick comes out dry when inserted in the center of the cake.

13. Cool to use immediately or wrap tightly to store.

# Angel Food Cake

It's easier than you think to make an angel food cake.
Even without sugar or wheat, this cake comes out very true to its name.

⅓ cup gluten-free flour blend
½ cup tapioca flour or cornstarch
⅓ cup almond flour (ground almonds)
⅛-¼ teaspoon pure stevia powder
¾ cup erythritol
12 egg whites
1½ teaspoons cream of tartar
2 teaspoons vanilla

1. Preheat the oven to 325°.

2. Whisk together the flours, stevia, and erythritol.

3. In a large bowl, beat the egg whites until foamy.

4. Beat in the cream of tartar.

5. Continue beating until stiff peaks form.

6. Beat in the vanilla.

7. With a sifter or strainer, dust the whites with ⅓ of the flour mixture. Gently fold in the flour.

8. Repeat two more times, folding just enough to incorporate the flour.

9. Spread the batter in an ungreased tube pan.

10. Bake 40-45 minutes until lightly brown and slightly firm.

11. Remove from the oven and invert on a rack until the cake is cool.

# Trifle

Trifle features fresh spring and summer fruits, layered with cake and custard.
Classically served in a cylindrical glass dish to show off the layers, it can
also be presented in goblets or parfait glasses.

## Custard Cream

2 tablespoons cornstarch or tapioca flour

½ teaspoon salt

⅛ teaspoon pure stevia powder

2½ cups milk (dairy, nut, coconut), divided

¼ cup yacon syrup or erythritol

4 egg yolks

⅛ teaspoon almond extract

2 tablespoons butter or coconut oil

## Fruit Mixture

1 cup blueberries

1 cup sliced strawberries, or raspberries

2 nectarines or peaches, sliced

(Or kiwi, papaya, mango or grapes)

## Cake

Use either the Sponge Cake from
page 84 or the Coconut Cake from page 88.

1. In a small saucepan, whisk together the cornstarch, salt and stevia.

2. Beat in 1½ cups of the milk and the yacon or erythritol.

3. Heat slowly, whisking constantly until mixture starts to thicken. Turn off the heat.

4. In a medium sized bowl, beat the yolks, almond extract and the other cup of milk.

5. Pour ⅓ of the heated milk mixture into the eggs, whisking constantly.

6. Pour egg mixture back into the saucepan and continue cooking and whisking until the custard thickens.

7. Add the butter, cut into pieces, and stir until it melts.

8. Pour into a bowl, cover, and cool the custard.

## To Assemble the Trifle

1. Spoon some custard into the bottom of a trifle dish or goblet.

2. Slice the cake and lay it on the custard.

3. Spoon on some fruit mixture.

4. Repeat these layers one or two more times and serve.

# Fruit Crisp

*The sauce adds an extra dimension of creaminess to the fruit layer to offset the crunch of the topping.*

**Filling**

2 tablespoons arrowroot powder, kuzu,
   or cornstarch
Pinch salt
1/8 teaspoon pure stevia powder
1 cup water
1/4 cup butter or coconut oil
2 teaspoons vanilla
2 teaspoons lemon zest (optional)
4 cups fruit (berries, sliced apples, rhubarb,
   peaches)

**Topping**

1/2 cup quinoa flakes or gluten-free rolled oats
1/2 cup gluten-free flour blend
1/2 teaspoon salt
1/8 teaspoon pure stevia powder
1/2 teaspoon cinnamon
1/4 cup ground flax seeds or almonds (optional)
1/3 cup butter, margarine, or coconut oil
1/4 cup finely chopped dates or raisins (optional)

1. Preheat the oven to 375°.
2. In a small saucepan, combine the arrowroot, kuzu or cornstarch, salt, and stevia.
3. Add the water and cook over medium heat, whisking constantly until it starts to thicken.
4. Remove from the heat.
5. Add the butter or coconut oil, vanilla and zest.
6. If using apples or peaches, peel them.
7. Chop or slice larger fruit.
8. In a mixing bowl, stir the sauce into the fruit.
9. Spread the fruit mixture into a medium-sized casserole dish.

**Topping**

1. Mix all ingredients except butter in a medium-sized bowl.
2. Melt the butter and stir into the dry ingredients.
3. Sprinkle topping over the fruit.
4. Bake for 45 minutes.

# Coconut Cake or Cupcakes

*Rich and quite moist, this cake stores well, but who can resist eating it?*

2 cups gluten-free flour blend
2 teaspoons baking powder
½ teaspoon baking soda
½ teaspoon salt
¼ teaspoon pure stevia powder
½ cup erythritol
2 egg whites
½ cup butter, margarine, oil or coconut oil
2 teaspoons vanilla
1 ¼ cups low-fat coconut milk

I. Preheat the oven to 350°.

2. In a large bowl, sift or whisk the flour, baking powder, baking soda, salt, stevia, and erythritol.

3. Beat the egg whites until foamy.

4. Add the well-softened butter and vanilla, beating well.

5. Beat in ⅓ of the coconut milk.

6. Beat in ⅓ of the dry ingredients.

7. Repeat 2 more times ending with the dry ingredients.

8. Grease or line muffin or cake pans.

9. Fill with the batter. Fill muffin cups ⅔ full.

IO. Bake cupcakes 20-25 minutes and the cake 35 minutes or until a toothpick inserted in the center comes out dry.

II. When cool spread with the following frosting.

## Coconut Buttercream Frosting

1½ tablespoons cornstarch or tapioca flour
Large pinch pure stevia powder
2 tablespoons erythritol
½ cup coconut milk
½ cup soft butter, margarine, or coconut butter
1 teaspoon vanilla
½ cup fine-shred unsweetened coconut
Coconut flakes for garnish (optional)

1. In a small heavy saucepan, stir together the cornstarch, stevia, and erythritol.

2. Add the coconut milk, whisking constantly and heating gently until it thickens.

3. Cool thoroughly.

4. Add the butter and vanilla and beat well.

5. Stir in the fine-shred coconut.

6. Frost your cake or cupcakes and garnish with coconut flakes if desired.

# Apple Tarts

Instead of tarts, you can use this recipe for an apple pie.

## Crust

1 cup gluten-free flour blend

Pinch salt

½ cup butter, margarine or coconut oil

2 tablespoons ice water

## Filling

4 firm apples

4 tablespoons butter

2 tablespoons lemon juice

1 teaspoon cinnamon

⅛ teaspoon pure stevia powder

½ cup yacon syrup

1 teaspoon vanilla

## Crust

1. By hand or in a food processor with the S blade, mix the flour and salt.

2. Cut in the butter to coarse crumbs.

3. Add the ice water and stir or pulse until barely mixed.

4. Line muffin or tart pans with muffin cups.

5. Divide the dough into 6-8 pieces and press each ball in the bottom of a muffin cup.

## Filling

1. Peel the apples and cut them into quarters.

2. Core each quarter and cut it into ¼-inch slices.

3. In a large heavy skillet, heat the butter, lemon juice, cinnamon, stevia, and yacon. Add apples.

4. Cook over medium heat, uncovered, for about 10 minutes, stirring often, to soften the apples and reduce the liquid.

5. Take the apples off the heat and add the vanilla.

6. Spoon the filling evenly onto the crusts.

7. Make crumb topping on the following page.

## Crumb Topping

1½ cups quinoa flakes or gluten-free rolled oats
⅛ teaspoon pure stevia powder
Pinch salt
¼ cup erythritol (optional)
6 tablespoons butter, margarine or coconut oil,
   melted

1. Preheat the oven to 375°.

2. Stir together the quinoa flakes or oats, stevia, salt and erythritol.

3. Stir in the butter.

4. Sprinkle topping over the apples, patting lightly.

5. Bake at 375° for ten minutes.

6. Reduce temperature to 350° and continue baking for another 30 minutes.

7. When cool, carefully lift each tart out of the pan.

8. Slide tarts out of muffin cups and serve.

# Lemon Cakes with Chevre

Some fresh thyme leaves add a new dimension to this easy and elegant dessert.

2 eggs, separated
Pinch salt
8 ounces plain chevre (goat cheese)
2 tablespoons erythritol
Pinch pure stevia powder
2 tablespoons gluten-free flour blend
Grated zest of 2 small lemons
Butter or oil for greasing muffin pans
1 pint fresh berries for topping

1. Preheat the oven to 350°.
2. Add salt to egg whites and whip to soft peaks.
3. Beat together until creamy the yolks, chevre, erythritol, stevia, flour blend and zest.
4. Fold 1/3 of the whites into the yolk mixture.
5. Fold the remaining whites into the yolk mixture.
6. Fill buttered or oiled muffin pans 2/3 full.
7. Bake 15-20 minutes.
8. Cool and remove from pans.
9. Top with fresh raspberries or other berries.

# Fresh Fig Tart

This tart is stunning to present. It features a remarkable array of flavors.

## Crust

1 cup walnuts
½ cup gluten-free flour blend
2 teaspoons rosemary
⅛ teaspoon pure stevia powder
⅛ cup erythritol
6 tablespoons butter
1 egg

## Cheese layer

12 oz chevre
½ cup yogurt or sour cream
¼ cup erythritol
⅛ teaspoon stevia
Zest of 1 large lemon

## Topping

1 lb fresh black mission figs
¼ cup yacon syrup
1 teaspoon balsamic vinegar

## Crust

1. Preheat the oven to 350°.
2. In a processor, pulse the nuts with the S-blade.
3. Add flour, rosemary, stevia, erythritol and pulse to mix.
4. Add butter and egg and pulse again just enough to mix.
5. Press dough into the bottom of an 8 or 9-inch spring-form pan.
6. Bake 20-25 minutes or until lightly browned.
7. When cool, remove the pan ring and set the crust on a large plate.

## Topping

1. Whisk together the chevre, yogurt or sour cream, erythritol, stevia and lemon zest.
2. Spread cheese mixture over the cooled crust.
3. Remove stems from the figs and slice into ¼-inch slices.
4. Arrange slices overlapping in circles on the cheese layer.
5. Stir together the yacon syrup and balsamic vinegar.
6. Spoon over the figs and serve.

# raw desserts

Don't miss the raw
cheesecakes in the
Beginning Recipes. Raw
desserts are guaranteed to
make you swoon.

## Ingredients for Raw Desserts

If you decide to become a raw chef, you will be contributing to your own and your loved ones' health, while enjoying delicious dishes that will astound you. In fact, you just can't believe it until you try them. When food is not heated, it comes to you in its natural state, bursting with flavor and nutrients. Instead of feeling full and drowsy, the raw food fills you with energy and clarity. Once you have your kitchen set up, it's really quite easy to make raw desserts. You'll save on energy costs, as there is no cooking.

With the raw foods movement in full swing, it's getting easier to find the necessary ingredients. A Vita Mix™ blender will really help with these desserts, as well as countless other kitchen tasks. A good blender is needed for the raw pies. If you decide to make the biscotti, you'll need a dehydrator. I recommend the Excalibur™ brand.

Below are some foods to gather for your Raw Dessert Kitchen. You can find many of them at larger health-conscious markets, or it's easy to order online. Study the ingredients, so you'll understand how to use them. Don't be intimidated by this list; it is comprehensive, in case you want to make all of the recipes, which you most likely will, once you taste them!

### Agar

A seaweed gelatin used to thicken raw desserts, agar is sold dried as powder or flakes. I use flakes in my recipes, so if you have powder, use half as much. Agar can be simmered in water, but for 100% raw desserts, it is blended with liquid on high speed until it warms and thickens.

### Cacao

Raw chocolate, called cacao, grows in the rainy parts of South America. Its botanical name, theobromine, means "food of the gods." The beans on the inside of the chocolate pod are used in many ways around the world. At one time cacao was used as currency. Raw cacao, high in antioxidants, is also a good source of magnesium to support the heart. Long known as an aphrodisiac, it elevates mood. Raw cacao is not heated but is fermented to get rid of some bitterness. You can find cacao as whole beans, nibs, powder or butter (the extracted fat solids.)

### Carob

Ground carob pods have a naturally sweet, chocolate taste. Most carob is roasted to give it a nuttier flavor. Truly raw carob tastes slightly chalky, so you may prefer the toasted carob, unless you are 100% raw. See p. 111 for ordering.

### Coconut butter

Sold in jars in many markets, this is coconut oil blended with coconut meat. A very nutritious food, it has many uses. For a simple treat spread some on a slice of apple. Blended with water, it makes raw coconut milk. My favorite brand is Artisana™. Look for it in many markets or see p. 111 for ordering.

### Coconut oil

Extracted from fresh coconuts, coconut oil is rich in healthy medium-chain fats. In addition to its great nutrition, coconut oil helps to rid the body of yeasts, fungus, and bacteria. Look for virgin or extra virgin coconut oil. It makes a superior skin lotion, too. Coconut oil is solid at room temperature, but liquefies easily when the jar is placed into a bowl of warm water. Check your local market or p. 111 for ordering.

### Goji berries

Also known as wolfberries, these nutritious fruits are high in protein and low on the glycemic index. Grown at high altitudes in remote, fertile regions of Asia, they have antioxidant properties and also strengthen the body. Look for dehydrated, untreated whole berries, which are more pure than the extracted juice. Check your local market or p. 111 for ordering.

### Irish moss

A seaweed gelatin, much like agar, used to help raw pies and puddings set up, Irish moss needs less blending time than agar. The best is sold whole and dried. See p. 111 for ordering.

To prepare Irish moss: Weigh out what the recipe calls for before soaking. Fill a bowl with clean water and soak Irish moss for at least 24 hours. Drain and refill the water several times to get out all the sand and debris. Drain and use in the recipes.

To prepare a whole package: Clean and soak the entire package. Blend the cleaned Irish moss with a small amount of water and freeze in ice cube trays. From an 8-ounce bag, make 16 ice cubes, so each cube will contain ½ ounce of seaweed. Thaw and use in the recipes.

### Kuzu (Kudzu) Root

This fleshy root is used as a thickener. Kuzu is sold dried in small bags in some markets . P. 111

has choices for ordering. It dissolves easily and needs to be blended on high long enough to heat up a bit.

### Maca root

From South America, maca has been used for thousands of years to balance hormones, supply minerals and elevate mood. It also improves energy, stamina and memory. For these recipes, look for bags of maca root powder. If you've never used maca, start with small amounts, as it is quite energizing. Ask for maca at your market or check p. 111 for ordering.

### Mesquite powder

Long used by indigenous peoples of the Americas as a sweetener, flour or fermented beverage, mesquite gives a nutty, smoky flavor to dishes. Look for it in health-conscious markets or check p. 111 for ordering.

### Young coconuts

These nutritional powerhouses come from Thailand and are found in the produce sections of larger natural food stores or Asian markets. About the size of a cantaloupe, they are covered with a white husk, which needs to be cut away to expose the nut. Unfortunately, it's almost impossible to find them organic, and there's some concern that they may be soaked in formaldehyde. Body Ecology™ now sells frozen coconut meat. See p. 111 for ordering.

To open the coconuts: Working on a steady surface (I do it in my sink), with a sharp knife, cut away the white husk from the top third of the coconut. With the back of a heavy knife or a cleaver, hit the coconut firmly about two inches from the top, working in a circle. BE CAREFUL. Keep turning and hitting it, and eventually you'll see a crack begin to form. Insert a knife and lift up the top. Drain the water into a clean bowl or measuring cup. With a large spoon, scrape the flesh from the shell, being careful to pick out any pieces of shell that come out with the flesh. Put the meat in a separate bowl.

You can also find raw confections in the Beginning Recipes and the Confections sections of the book.

# Nectarine Dream Cream

This raw pudding is so light.
Yogurt or kefir can replace the fresh coconut milk.

1½ tablespoons agar flakes

1 tablespoon kuzu root (or 1 oz. of Irish moss to replace agar and kuzu)

1 cup almond milk

1 cup fresh coconut milk

2 nectarines, pitted and chopped

2 teaspoons vanilla

1/8 teaspoon pure stevia powder

¼ cup yacon syrup

2 teaspoons lemon juice

6 tablespoons coconut butter

1. Mix the agar and kuzu with the almond milk in a Vita Mix™ or heavy-duty blender.

2. Cover tightly and blend on high until it thickens. (1-2 minutes.)

3. To make fresh coconut milk, see directions under young coconuts above. (Or blend ¼ cup coconut butter with ¾ cup water.)

4. Blend in the rest of the ingredients until the mixture is creamy.

5. Pour into bowls or glasses and chill at least 4 hours.

6. Garnish with a little freshly-grated nutmeg, if desired.

# Lemon Dream Cream

A sweet-tart version of Dream Cream—it's a raw dessert soufflé.

1 young coconut
1 rounded tablespoon kuzu root
1 rounded tablespoon agar flakes
Juice of 1 large or 2 small lemons
A few drops lemon oil or extract (optional)
¼ cup yacon syrup or 3 soaked dates
⅛ teaspoon stevia
Pinch turmeric for color
⅓ cup coconut butter

1. See page 98 for opening young coconuts.
2. Mix 1½ cups of the coconut water with the kuzu and agar in a heavy-duty blender.
3. Cover and blend on high until the mixture thickens.
4. Add the other ingredients and blend until smooth and creamy.
5. Pour into glasses or bowls.
6. Cover and chill at least 4 hours to let it thicken.

# Raw Chocolate Pudding

We all have memories of chocolate pudding, right?
This one is light and delectable. Guaranteed guilt-free.

3½ cups nut or coconut milk, divided
1 tablespoon kuzu
 2 tablespoons agar flakes
½ cup yacon syrup or 6 chopped dates
⅛ teaspoon pure stevia powder
2 teaspoons alcohol-free vanilla
½ cup cacao powder
Pinch salt
1 tablespoon mesquite powder (optional)
⅓ cup coconut butter

1. In a blender, mix 1 cup of nut milk with the kuzu and agar.

2. Blend on high speed until the mixture gets warm and thickens.

3. (Or substitute 1 oz. of Irish moss and blend just until smooth.)

4. Add the rest of the ingredients and blend until smooth.

5. Pour into bowls or goblets and let cool at least 3 hours.

# Raw Key Lime Pie

Avocados give creaminess and healthy fats to the base of this traditional favorite.
Be sure to add more stevia if you want the filling sweeter.

## Crust

1¼ cups almond meal
1¼ cups fine shred unsweetened coconut
Pinch pure stevia powder
Pinch salt
3 tablespoons coconut oil
½ teaspoon vanilla
4 tablespoons almond or coconut milk

## Filling

¾ cup lime juice
1 rounded tablespoon lime zest
3 large or 5 small avocados, cut into
    chunks
¼-½ cup yacon syrup or 6 soaked dates
¼ teaspoon pure stevia powder
Pinch salt
½ cup coconut butter

## Crust

1. To make your own almond meal, grind whole or blanched almonds in a processor or coffee grinder.

2. Set the jar of coconut oil in hot water to soften.

3. Stir together or process crust ingredients.

4. Rub a pie pan with coconut oil.

5. Press the dough firmly into the pan.

## Filling

1. In a Vita Mix™ or heavy-duty blender, blend filling ingredients to a smooth consistency. Mixture will be thick.

2. Taste and correct for sweetness.

3. Pour the filling into the crust and spread.

4. Chill at least 4 hours.

5. Top with meringue if desired.

## Meringue

1 tablespoon agar flakes
1 tablespoon kuzu
Water and meat of 1 young coconut
    ( see p. 98)
½ cup cashews, soaked ½ hour and drained
1 teaspoon vanilla
¼ teaspoon pure stevia powder
¼ cup yacon syrup (or 4 dates, chopped fine)
½ cup coconut butter

I.  Blend on high speed 1 cup of coconut water with the agar and kuzu until warm and thick.

2.  Add the other ingredients and blend on high until smooth.

3.  Refrigerate meringue at least 2 hours before topping the pie.

# Raw Cacao–Banana Cream Pie

Better than a banana split—and definitely healthier.
Top with some Raw Chocolate Sauce from page 109.

## Crust

½ cup almond flour (ground almonds)
½ cup cacao powder
Pinch salt
½ cup fine-shred unsweetened coconut
⅛ teaspoon pure stevia powder
2 tablespoons yacon syrup
2 tablespoons softened coconut oil
2 tablespoons nut milk

## Filling

2 cups almond or coconut milk, divided
1 cup cashews
2 tablespoons agar flakes
1 tablespoon kuzu root
1 cup fine-shred coconut
⅓ cup yacon syrup (or 4 dates)
2 small or 1 large banana
3 teaspoons alcohol-free vanilla
6 tablespoons coconut butter
2 additional bananas, for slicing

## Crust

1. Mix the almonds, cacao, salt, coconut, and stevia together in a bowl or food processor.

2. Combine the yacon, coconut oil and almond milk.

3. Mix everything together until dough forms.

4. Rub a pie pan with a little coconut oil and press in the crust, working it up the sides.

## Filling

1. Soak the cashews in 1 cup milk for at least 20 minutes.

2. Meanwhile in a high-powered blender, on high, blend the other cup of almond milk with the agar and kuzu until it's thick.

3. Add the cashews, yacon, bananas, vanilla and coconut butter, blending until smooth and creamy.

4. Spread the sliced bananas on the pie shell.

5. Pour the filling over the bananas.

6. Freeze the pie for 1 hour, then refrigerate until set.

7. Drizzle chocolate sauce (p. 109) on the whole pie or on individual pieces.

# Raw Pumpkin Pie

*Without cooking, you get all the minerals, vitamins and antioxidants
of the squash and the same—or better—sweet taste.*

## Crust

2 cups pecans or walnuts

Pinch salt

4-6 dates, pitted and chopped

2 teaspoons vanilla

## Filling

1 tablespoon kuzu root

2 tablespoons agar flakes

1 cup water or nut milk

½ cup cashews soaked 2 hours in ¼ cup water

3 cups butternut squash, peeled, seeded and cubed

¼ cup yacon syrup or 4 soaked dates

⅛ teaspoon pure stevia powder

2 teaspoons vanilla

2 teaspoons cinnamon

1 teaspoon ground ginger

½ teaspoon nutmeg

⅛ teaspoon cloves

½ cup coconut butter

## Crust

1. In a food processor with the S blade, grind the nuts with the salt.

2. Add the dates and vanilla and process until dough sticks together.

3. Press into a pie pan, working it up the sides.

## Filling

1. In a high-powered blender, blend the kuzu and agar with the water or nut milk on high speed until thickened.

2. Add the other ingredients and blend until smooth. (You may use 4 teaspoons pumpkin pie spice instead of the individual spices).

3. Pour the filling into the piecrust.

4. Chill overnight or put the pie in the freezer for 1 hour, then in the refrigerator for at least 6 hours.

5. Top with meringue from p. 103 if desired.

# Raw Coconut Cream Pie

*This was the first raw pie I ever made.*
*I knew right away that raw pies were the ultimate dessert treat.*

**Crust**

1 cup shredded coconut

1 cup almond flour (ground almonds)

Pinch salt

Pinch stevia

3 tablespoons coconut oil

1 teaspoon vanilla

¼ cup coconut or almond milk

**Filling**

2 cups coconut water, divided

1 tablespoon kuzu root

2 tablespoons agar flakes or use 1½ oz. of Irish moss for the kuzu and agar. See page 97

Meat of 2 young coconuts

½ cup cashew pieces, soaked 1 hour in ½ cup coconut water

1 teaspoon vanilla

⅛ teaspoon pure stevia powder

½ cup coconut butter

¼ cup yacon syrup or 4 soaked dates

**Garnish**

¼ cup shredded or flaked coconut

**Crust**

1. If using coconut milk, save ¼ cup from what you make for the filling to use in the crust.

2. Mix the coconut, almond flour, salt, and stevia together by hand or in a processor.

3. Soften the coconut oil by putting the jar into a dish of warm water and pouring off 3 tablespoons of the oil.

4. Mix the oil with the vanilla and coconut milk.

5. Stir this into the dry ingredients by hand or with the processor.

6. Rub a pie pan with coconut oil and press the crust into the pan, working it up the sides.

**Filling**

1. In a Vita Mix™ or heavy-duty blender, combine 1 cup of the coconut water, the kuzu and agar.

2. Cover and blend on high speed until the mixture gets warm and thickens. (Omit this step if using Irish moss.)

3. Add the rest of the ingredients and blend until smooth.

4. Pour the filling into the piecrust. Garnish with coconut.

5. Freeze 1 hour, then refrigerate until set.

# Dehydrated Chocolate Cinnamon Biscotti

If you don't have a dehydrator yet, get one so you can try these biscotti.
They are packed with flavor and nutrients.

3 cups almond flour (ground almonds)
½ cup cacao powder (or carob)
⅛-¼ teaspoon pure stevia powder
1 tablespoon cinnamon
Pinch salt
1½ cups unsweetened shredded coconut
½ cup cacao nibs
4 large apples or pears, cored and chopped
⅓ cup yacon syrup

(If you're making your own ground almonds, use the blender or food processor with the S blade. They should be fine, but not buttery.)

1. In a large bowl, stir together the almond flour, cacao, stevia, cinnamon, salt, coconut, and nibs.

2. Puree the apples or pears in a processor.

3. Add the fruit and yacon to the nut mixture. Stir well.

4. On a clean cutting surface form ½ of the dough into a loaf, 2½ inches wide and 1 inch high. (If dough is too wet to work with, cover and leave it for ½ to 1 hour while it firms up.)

5. With a wide knife, slice off a ½-inch piece. Tip the knife to pick up the biscotti, using your fingers to hold it while you transfer it to a dehydrator tray.

6. Repeat with the rest of the loaf.

7. Form the remaining dough into a loaf and slice.

8. Dehydrate at 145° for 1 hour—NO LONGER!

9. Lower the heat to 105° and continue dehydrating until the cookies are crunchy. This may take up to 24 hours.

10. Pack cooled biscotti into airtight containers. Biscotti keep well in the freezer.

# Dehydrated Cranberry Biscotti

These cookies turn out a beautiful pink color and have a lot of zing.

1½ cups almonds, ground
3 cups fine-shred coconut
⅛-¼ teaspoon pure stevia powder
4 pears, cored (or apples)
½ fresh pineapple or 1 package frozen, thawed
1 inch piece of fresh ginger (optional)
1 package fresh or frozen cranberries

1. In a food processor with the S-blade, grind the almonds until fine.

2. In a large bowl, combine the almonds, coconut, and stevia.

3. Puree the pears, pineapple, and ginger and add to the nut mixture.

4. Process the cranberries until chopped fine, but not mushy. Add to the dough.

5. If the dough seems too wet to shape and slice, cover and leave it for ½ −1 hour to set up.

6. Refer to steps 5−10 in the preceding recipe for cutting and dehydrating.

# Raw Chocolate Sauce

You'll find yourself pouring it on everything!

1½ cups almond milk (or other nut milk)
¾ cup cacao or carob powder
⅛ teaspoon pure stevia powder
2 tablespoons yacon syrup (or 5 chopped dates)
1 tablespoon alcohol-free vanilla
Pinch salt
2 teaspoons mesquite powder (optional)
2 tablespoons coconut butter

1. Blend all ingredients until smooth.

2. Mesquite gives a rich flavor to the sauce.

3. The sauce will gradually thicken.

So prized was the cocoa bean that some ancient South American cultures used it as currency.

# Raw Coconut Ice Cream

Homemade ice cream is easy to make. Eat it while it's still soft.

1 tablespoon agar flakes

Meat and water of 2 young coconuts (see page 98)

1 inch piece of vanilla bean or 2 teaspoons vanilla

1/8 teaspoon pure stevia powder

Pinch salt

1/2 cup shredded dried coconut (optional)

1.  Blend the agar with 1 cup coconut water on high until thickened.

2.  Add the other ingredients and blend.

3.  Freeze in an ice cream freezer.

4.  For a sweeter ice cream, blend in a few chopped dates.

# Raw Cashew Vanilla Ice Cream

How about this ice cream with a Dehydrated Chocolate Cinnamon Biscotti and some Raw Chocolate Sauce?

4 cups nut milk or water

1 tablespoon agar flakes

2 cups cashews

1/8 teaspoon pure stevia powder

1/3 cup yacon syrup or 4 chopped dates

1 tablespoon vanilla

1.  Blend 1 cup of nut milk with the agar on high until thickened.

2.  Add the other ingredients and blend until smooth.

3.  Freeze in an ice cream freezer.

# Resources

**Carob powder**
www.organiclivingfood.com

**Coconut butter** (Artisana)
www.premierorganics.org

**Coconut oil**
www.organiclivingfood.com
www.premierorganics.org

**Erythritol**
www.asweetlifewithoutsugar.com

**Gogi berries**
www.ForGojiBerries.com
www.organiclivingfood.com
www.navitasnaturals.com

**Irish Moss**
www.transitionnutrition.com

**Kuzu root**
www.amazon.com
www.tropicaltraditions.com

**Maca**
www.organiclivingfood.com
www.navitasnaturals.com

**Mesquite powder**
www.livingtreecommunity.com

**Stevia, pure white extract**
www.asweetlifewithoutsugar.com

**Yacon syrup**
www.asweetlifewithoutsugar.com

**Young coconut meat**
www.bodyecology.com

## Recipe Index